Software Quality and Copyright:

Issues in Computer-Assisted Instruction

Virginia Helm

Association for Educational Communications & Technology
1126 Sixteenth Street, N.W., Washington, D.C. 20036

Library of Congress Catalog Card No. 84-81566
ISBN 0-89240-047-1
Printed in the United States of America

Published and Distributed by:
Association for Educational Communications and Technology
1126 16th Street NW
Washington, D.C. 20036

CONTENTS

ACKNOWLEDGEMENTS

I am indebted to numerous people who willingly gave of their time while I plied them with questions about legal or technological aspects of computing in the educational setting. My colleagues, Charles Clark and Marilyn Ward, both contributed to educating me about the intricacies of the topic: Chuck's knowledge about microcomputers and especially about networking in a school environment is seemingly unlimited; Marilyn's expertise with instructional software and evaluation simplified my task. Michael Keplinger in the Copyright Office provided invaluable assistance by referring me to the most noted authorities in the field of computer copyright law; their informal opinions provided the basis for the legal analysis in chapters three and four. To my husband, Tom, who relinquished his access time to our own micro for the duration of this writing project—as well as entertaining our two-year-old for those essential evenings and week-ends of writing—I am deeply indebted until such point in the imminent future when I will be repaying the debt in kind. I cannot resist acknowledging my MORROW DESIGNS microcomputer, a superb machine without which the deadlines for this monograph simply could not have been met. And in the honorable tradition of "last but not least" I wish to express my appreciation to the editorial staff at AECT, whose enthusiasm, creativity and competence are every writer's dream.

Virginia Helm
Western Illinois University

PREFACE

As the number of computers in schools has increased, quality in the production of instructional computer software has become a major issue. How that quality can be improved is the subject of much debate, as is the issue of software piracy, which seriously threatens the software market.

The quality issue has given rise to two camps: the few who maintain that available software is about as good as current technology—and the marketplace—will produce, and the many who believe that software quality can be substantially improved. Educators tend to blame software producers for alleged poor quality; producers blame educators for not using existing software to capacity, for not demanding better programs, and for pirating away profits that could be used to enhance the product.

Throughout the controversy that has ebbed and flowed between users and producers, and across the software industry, one thing has been apparent: few educators and producers talk to one another in reasoned tones about quality or copyright. Dialogue between industry spokespersons and educators experienced in software use has simply not occurred, depriving us of a major resource for resolving issues of national concern.

As an organization of both producers and users of educational software, the Association for Educational Communications and Technology (AECT) has been acutely aware of the need for such constructive interchange. This need was also noted by the National Institute of Education (NIE).

From discussions between the leadership of the NIE and AECT

came the conclusion that these organizations together could play an effective role as catalyst in generating a productive dialogue between producers and users of instructional software. Following early discussions in June of 1983, a September date was selected for a National Conference on Producer-Educator Perspectives on Educational Software. Invitations were sent by NIE Director Manuel J. Justiz to presentors and participants. Most eagerly accepted. Invitational papers were commissioned from Daniel T. Brooks, nationally-prominent software copyright attorney, and LaRuth Morrow, a consultant on computer software from Richardson, Texas.

Representing software producers at the conference were Charles Blashke, president of Education Turnkey Systems; Peter Dublin, president of Intentional Education; Tory Esbenson, president of Micro-Ed; Terry Gilbreth, director of electronic and media publishing for the School Publishing Division of CBS; Jeanne Gleason, editor of *Electronic Publishing* for the Silver-Burdett Company; Bodie Marx, vice president of the computer software division of The Milliken Company; and Preston Stone of the Education Division of the Tandy (Radio Shack) Corporation.

Those speaking for education and training were Dan Dearborn, assistant superintendent of Alexandria (Virginia) City Public Schools; Dan Dolan, specialist in mathematics and computer education for the Montana Office of Public Instruction; Bobby Goodson, president of Computer Using Educators (CUE) of California; Richard A. Pollack of the Minnesota Educational Computing Consortium (MECC); Alex Sanchez, associate provost for community education of the University of New Mexico; and Warren Spurlin, deputy superintendent of Sarasota (Florida) County Schools.

The AECT participated in planning the conference and arranged for sessions to be videotaped. The Association's leadership determined that the subjects of software quality and copyright were of sufficient professional interest to justify the production of a book on these timely topics. Careful documentation to support or contradict general perceptions would be extremely helpful to the field, Association leaders reasoned. The conference was seen as an unprecedented vehicle for bringing to light all viewpoints essential for a thorough and scholarly treatment of the subjects of quality and copyright.

Selection of an author with the requisite background in education, copyright law, and familiarity with software issues to review and integrate the conference information seemed at first a virtually impossible task. The field is so new and laws as yet so untested that few professionals exist who have acquired the necessary experience and skill to deal with the thorny issues of copyright and quality. But then we found Virginia Helm.

Helm is associate professor of educational administration at Western Illinois University, where she teaches school law. Her recent (1982) doctorate in administration was completed at the University of Iowa, where she became interested in the use of computers in the classroom. Much of the early research and development in computer-assisted instruction occurred at the University of Iowa, and to this day, it is noted as a leading university in applying computers to teaching and learning.

Following the September conference, Virginia Helm diligently applied herself to analyzing the legal and extralegal claims and motivations of conference presentors and participants. In examining the quality issue, she talked not only with those who attended the national conference, but also with numerous luminaries noted by presentors or cited in the literature. She also consulted with many software producers, both those in attendance at the conference and those significantly involved in the market.

In investigating the copyright issue, Helm not only relied on Daniel Brooks, but also tracked down those attorneys involved in the legislative history of the 1980 computer copyright amendment to the 1976 Copyright Act, particularly those who had experience with the law as it applied to instructional software. Through references from colleagues and the literature, she contacted nearly a dozen nationally-prominent copyright attorneys who are familiar with issues of software copyright. Her goal, which she has clearly achieved, was to describe the state of the art of the production of instructional software and its protection through copyright law.

We are indebted to Tom Asick, NIE conference coordinator, and to those producers and educators who so selflessly presented and participated in the national software conference and to those who cooperated with us in the development and production of this work. All of us are hopeful that this volume, developed through the collaboration of the public and private sectors, will contribute helpfully to the improvement of educational software and to a better understanding—by producers and users as well as legal and legislative personnel—of American copyright law as it is construed and applied to instructional software. This book will facilitate the evolution of instructional software as a means for improving the education and training of our nation's citizens. We trust that it will contribute to all of our efforts to achieve excellence in American education.

Lyn Gubser, Ph.D.
Executive Director
Association for Educational
  Communications & Technology
Washington, D.C.

January 30, 1984

Paul Resta, Ph.D.
Chief of Planning, Research,
  and Technology
National Institute of Education
Washington, D.C.

CHAPTER 1

INTRODUCTION

The world of modern technology was ruled until recently by the heavy, often dirty, machines carrying out the mechanical functions of industrial production. That reign ended with accession to the technological throne of the computer with its immaculate, electronic processes of information mangement. In both instances, the public was inclined to perceive these machines as cold and impersonal, if not hostile to humanity. But these qualities were generally accepted as the price to be paid for levels of productivity and efficiency previously unimaginable.

If the computer has been for a couple of decades the reigning monarch of technology, the microcomputer is the newly arrived heir to the throne. Whether the micro is perceived as cold and impersonal, however, depends to some extent upon whether the perceivers are users or nonusers. The former are frequently so smitten by the computer's efficiency and addictive powers that they are prone to regard the popularly designed "personal computer" as just that: quite personal indeed.

The microcomputer, as the infant darling of technology and in fact of all society, may be receiving all of the attention and adoration reserved for royal heirs, but it is still an infant. As such, its functions remain limited, its movements uncoordinated, and its potential for growth immense but currently unrealized. In fact, what it will look and act like in its maturity is only hinted at in its current embodiment. What we can anticipate with certainty is an exciting growth in its capacity for efficiency and diversity of functions.

Government and business were among the first to be warmed by the glow of efficiency and productivity surrounding the computer and its users. During the fifties, sixties, and even into the seventies, only the larger institutions and organizations could afford the costly machine. Interestingly, there has been a consistent correlation between the size of the computer and the size of the institution utilizing it: the mammoth computers of the 1950s were so expensive that only the largest of governmental or business agencies could afford them; the briefcase-sized microcomputer of the 1980s is now affordable by anyone who can afford a good briefcase. Three decades ago, the computer market was limited to big business and big government. Today the computer industry is courting not only smaller units of government and business, but also the school and the home.

It is not surprising that business and industry should welcome the computer into their operations; efficiency and productivity, after all, are the key to profits. Nor is it surprising that individuals and families are responding to the multiple enticements of entertainment, education, and efficiency in managing their personal lives. Many educators, on the other hand, tend to be a bit skeptical—almost nervous—about the invasion of the computer into their domain. Teachers wonder whether the computer might simply be the latest in a long string of expensive technological wonders hawked by producers and glorified by educational "experts" for their capacity to revolutionize education: teaching machines, filmstrip projectors, film projectors, overhead projectors, educational television (both closed and open circuit), language labs for individualized learning, audio instruction, and information retrieval centers. What, they ask, makes the computer any different?

This world-weary cynicism, whether genuine or affected, is superficial in comparison to the deeper anxiety of many teachers that they can never successfully compete with the computer. They are little comforted by the assertions of the popular media that computers teach the basic skills no better than teachers using traditional methods [Waters, 1983; Mitgang, 1983]. What the typical media reporter has not yet discovered, of course, is the small but growing body of research on the effectiveness of computer-assisted instruction (CAI) [Kulik, 1983; White, 1983]. A vast majority of these studies indicate that when compared to traditional classroom instruction, computers improve both the level of achievement and the rate of learning for many students. Computers have been found to decrease learning time by anywhere from 30 percent to 88 percent, depending upon the type of student and the subject area or skills to be learned. Low and high achieving students (as opposed to "average" students) seem best able to benefit from computer-assisted instruction, and their improvement has been most dramatic in science, foreign language, and mathematics [Fisher, 1983].

What cannot but unnerve even the most adventuresome and self-confident teacher, however, is not the computer's efficiency in self-paced, individualized instruction, but its inherent ability to captivate students far beyond their usual limited attention spans. Such "performance" anxieties are seldom if ever discussed, perhaps because they are not even self-admitted. What is verbalized instead is a litany of the computer's deficiencies, most of which pertain to the poor quality of educational software being peddled to the schools.

Software developers and producers themselves readily admit that there is lamentable room for improvement in the quality of instructional programs now available for classroom use. Their own defense, however, is a counterattack. How can we, they ask, continue to invest the prodigious amounts of money required to develop and produce software for the schools when educators blatantly violate federal copyright law by making multiple copies from one purchased copy (pirating), or buying one disk, loading it sequentially into each of a dozen microcomputers in a classroom or lab so that twelve students are using that one copy, or by allowing twenty students to access one computer program through a microcomputer network? The school market is so small to begin with, they argue, that profits are likely to be quite limited. If schools cannot or will not pay for the copies they use, then producers cannot and will not pay for the continued development and production of instructional software for them.

As is often the case in education, money seems to be the crux of the problem. School districts cannot afford to buy at retail cost tens or hundreds of copies of each instructional program selected for their classrooms—nor would taxpayers want them to purchase such quantities at current prices! Commercial software producers, on the other hand, cannot be expected simply to donate their time and budgets to the schools. This perplexing dilemma is one that society has a vested interest in resolving. The quality of education, after all, has recently acquired the status of Most Favored Social Problem. In the development of our multifaceted strategy to raise the level of teaching and learning in the classroom, there is a vital role for computers. But the potential contribution of computers in this endeavor depends on the quality of the software available. For this reason society must do more than wait for educators and software producers to resolve their apparent conflict.

As with any complex problem, we must be sure that we fully understand the position of each interest group. Listening to both educators and software producers, we must be able to separate fact from fiction, accusation from indictment, and feasible goal from impossible dream. Our ability to make such judgments will depend upon our having assembled and assimilated sufficient data. We must also learn what specific deficiencies exist in educational software currently available, how extensive is the problem of software piracy, and what the federal copyright law actually allows and prohibits.

As crucial as is the dual problem of software quality and piracy, we need not necessarily panic over the possibility that software producers will stop creating instructional software before we can curb the piracy that they believe deprives them of their due profits. Both the problem of software quality and the problem of piracy are, to some extent, transitional problems. The metaphor of the infant—royal or otherwise—contains the essence of the complex problems surrounding the discussion of microcomputers in general and educational micros in particular. More specifically, microcomputer hardware and software are in the very early stages of development. As with any technological evolution, the first models or productions—wondrous though they may seem—are notoriously primitive by later standards. Just because many educational computer programs are unsophisticated or inadequate today doesn't mean that instructional software is inherently inferior. And just because schools may currently be using too many illegally copied computer programs doesn't mean that such piracy won't be curbed in the future, either by the schools themselves, by technology, or by some external monitoring agency.

Understanding the piracy and software quality problems as transitional or developmental must not, however, inure us to the urgency of resolving these issues. The educational system is perceived by many educators and lay people as laggard enough in meeting the needs of contemporary society. Failing to act quickly and intelligently to minimize the problems of piracy and software quality will only complicate the task of the schools as they try to raise their standards and performance levels. The action to be taken requires the commitment of all three sectors affected by the existence of the piracy and software quality problems: educators who need quality software at prices they can afford; software producers who need a reasonable return on their investments in creating the software; and society, which needs a strong, effective educational system to ensure continued economic, moral, and military strength.

We tend to be acclimated in our culture to expect current problems to be defined and analyzed in terms of crises, the instant and simple solution to which is imperative. And there are some who would describe the use of computers as the current "crisis in the classroom." The present discussion of computer software and copyright as they pertain to the schools, however, is founded upon the conviction that as serious as is the cluster of problems surrounding educational computing, those problems do not now constitute a crisis. If the sectors most concerned about preventing a crisis and solving current problems can understand that the limitations of the software and piracy problems are essentially the shortcomings of a newly developing product in its infancy, they may be able to work together with the patience and realistic expectations necessary to achieve the most effective solutions.

The chapters that follow present a description and analysis of the separate aspects of the two interconnected problems of educational software quality and piracy. Chapter two begins with an investigation of accusations regarding the alleged dismal quality of educational software. This necessitates a discussion of the deficiencies most frequently cited, which can be categorized into two main types of defects: technical or functional and pedagogical. That drill-and-practice programs bear the brunt of the criticism about software quality is only partly explained by the predominance of these programs in the larger market of instructional software. The large number of drill-and-practice programs attracts intense critical attention, which tends to highlight small flaws as well as major deficiencies. Exploring the reasons for the alleged dearth of high quality educational software, we must focus on drill-and-practice software and questions raised about its function in the classroom. Some of these questions in turn cause us to confront questions about the nature and purpose of education, about the role of computers in pursuing our educational goals, and about the past, present, and future roles of teachers in our educational system. Why the quality of instructional software is so problematic is a question that must also be addressed if progress is to be made in improving that quality. Educators and software producers provide different answers to this question. As we come to understand their respective insights, we begin to see the need to redefine the problem. Chapter two, then, closes with that redefinition.

Many software producers vehemently insist that piracy is a major factor accounting for their reluctance to invest in producing the quality of software educators want. We therefore will investigate the reality behind accusations of rampant piracy and the effect of piracy on the quality of instructional software. Documenting the extensiveness of piracy is difficult but not impossible, based on what is known by everyone with access to or experience with microcomputers: that what can be done with relative ease for considerable financial savings will be done, whether blatantly or surreptiously. But the ease with which most software can be copied (illegally) and the savings that accrue are only two of the reasons for the existence of piracy in the school setting. Educators' lack of knowledge about the copyright law and its implications for software usage also contribute to the piracy problem. Although some cynics might snicker at the suggestion, there are those who believe that if educators were more fully aware of the impact of copying and using illegally copied instructional programs, they would make a more concerted effort to abide by the law. For that reason much of chapter three focuses on what the copyright law says and how it is currently being interpreted nationally by copyright specialists. We shall see that the specific provisions of the law and its differing interpretations raise but leave unanswered a number of questions about educational uses of software in the schools.

Chapter four presents legal principles or tests that can be applied to determine the potential legality or illegality of such practices as networking or sequentially loading a series of computers from one floppy disk. Additionally, this chapter touches briefly on several other important concerns pertaining to software in school libraries, the differences between owning and leasing software, and the consequences of infringing the copyright law.

Chapter five focuses on the various means available to both educators and software producers, as well as to society, in their mutual efforts to contain or control illegal copying and the use of illegally copied software in the schools. Educators can pursue a variety of activities at the state and local levels to increase general awareness about copyright law and its implications for legal uses of instructional software. There are several approaches to controlling the use of software, among which we include self-monitoring and monitoring by state education agencies. Software producers can continue to search for effective technological solutions to the piracy problem, attempting to secure their programs mechanically from unapproved copying. They can also cooperate with educators in a variety of negotiated licensing and purchasing agreements that would greatly reduce the perceived "need" to engage in illegal copying in order to operate within strained school budgets. While most of the incentive and responsibility for resolving the piracy problem resides with educators and software producers, there is a potential and significant role for society, primarily through state and federal government. Some possible government actions are presented and discussed briefly.

In light of predictions on the part of some software producers and analysts [see Finkel, 1983] that piracy in the schools may result in a shift in emphasis from the school market to the home market, we will conclude by investigating some of the perceived threats to the school market for educational software. How real are these threats? And do nonprofit educational software producers offer a competitive challenge to commercial software producers? Will they address different educational markets, with nonprofit producers supplying the needs of smaller interest groups such as special education and bilingual education? When we raise questions about the future of the school market for commercial instructional software, are we not in fact raising questions about the future of the school market for all instructional software, irrespective of who produced it? These and related questions are the focus of the last chapter.

CHAPTER 2
THE PROBLEM OF QUALITY

IS IT A REAL PROBLEM? "The quality of most educational software is abysmal." This could well be the most frequently heard of casual assessments about the quality of instructional software. More formal assessments, pronounced by analysts with stature and experience in evaluating software, are typified by a mildly critical National Science Foundation report that found improvements in the present quality and effectiveness of educational software are needed. Carl Berger, a software evaluation expert at the University of Michigan, is both more specific and more critical. He maintains that five percent of the educational software currently on the market is excellent, 20 percent is good, and the remaining 75 percent is poor [Berger, 1983]. A harsher assessment, however, comes from industry spokesman Chuck Carlson of Random House, who claims that "[T]he figures that go around the industry are that only 3-5 percent of the educational programs that are available are worth looking at" [*Electronic Learning*, Nov./Dec. 1981, p. 34]. Surely, if software producers themselves willingly share such confessions, the litany of criticism repeated by many educators merits serious consideration.

Before listing and analyzing the common criticisms of today's educational software, it should be noted that much of that criticism is directed at software produced by or for the commercial market. With the profit motive as their primary incentive, many commercial developers have been understandably eager to take advantage of a market so new and so rapidly expanding that any program that could run was likely to be considered good—if only because it had little or no competition. Most programers, furthermore, had no educational training or experience, resulting in a multitude of instructional deficiencies. Educational programs designed by such nonprofit corporations as the Minnesota Educational Computing Consortium (MECC), on the other hand, are more likely to be the product of designers or programers with experience in the field of education. They are therefore less likely to exhibit the pedagogical deficiencies that often characterize commercially produced instructional software. For the very reason that they are not profit-driven, the not-for-profit education-related software producers can afford to devote the extra time and effort required to produce higher quality programs. Such broad generalizations are not meant to condemn all commercially produced educational software or to praise all noncommercially developed software. They do, however, suggest general tendencies that should be kept in mind as we look at the critique of educational software that follows.

COMMON CRITICISMS

What are the deficiencies most frequently identified by users and by professional evaluators of educational software? Numerous as the specific criticisms are, they tend to fall into two primary categories. The first category consists of deficiencies that are technological or functional in nature, that is, deficiencies or defects associated with the operation of the software as well as the extent to which programs utilize the potential contained in hardware. The second category includes deficiencies of a pedagogical nature. In this category we place concerns about learning theory, diagnostic and individualizing components, and the congruence of subject matter, mode of delivery, and developmental level of students. Some defects, of course, defy neat placement in one or the other category, containing elements of neither or both types of deficiencies.

Functional Deficiencies

Functional deficiencies include some of the most easily corrected defects in educational software. Spelling and grammatical errors are among the most simple—and inexcusable—but they occur with distressing frequency. They should be unacceptable at any time, but they are especially so now, given the national preoccupation with basics. Only slightly more complex are defects that prevent programs from loading easily or properly. Users, especially young ones, should be spared not only programs that are difficult to load, but also programs with a complicated procedure for entering answers. Once an answer has been entered, provisions should also be made for erasing or correcting that answer. This ability, believe it or not, is too often lacking in the educational software currently on the market.

An even more serious flaw involves programs in which a wrong answer brings the program to a complete halt. It is not uncommon to find programs in which a wrong answer brings no response—no directions for returning to the original question or for moving ahead to the next one—just a static screen to which the only logical (and usually frustrated) response is to shut off the computer. Good programs must include provisions for inappropriate responses, whether honest or intentionally experimental, so that the program either moves ahead or presents some kind of a "try again" message.

Another relatively simple functional problem is found in arithmetic programs designed to teach addition. As described in *Creative Computing* [Kleiman and others, p. 88]: "many addition programs present the problems with the addends side by side, require the answers to be entered from left to right, and do not provide any way of marking carrying. In using these programs, children often copy the problem, work it on paper, and then enter their answer into the computer." Such nonfunctional design is a major flaw from the perspective of the user, though seemingly minor from the standpoint of the producer responsible for correcting it.

One more example of an easily correctible, functional deficiency is the existence of a screen so densely packed with information that the user has neither the motivation nor the eye capacity to read and work with the information. Sophisticated designers and producers of print media publications are keenly aware of the impact of visual appearance in attracting and retaining a reader's attention. Spreads are carefully designed with an eye to balancing space, text, and pictures. Software designers need to be equally sensitive to the motivational impact of an attractive visual format, as well as to the importance of the motivational force of the material itself.

Poor quality of instructions contained within a given program constitutes another common functional deficiency—one that generates a high level of frustration for students and teachers alike. Clear, concise, and complete instructions within a program, i.e., those appearing on the monitor, are essential for the user. Too many programers, especially those without a teaching background, fail to understand or appreciate the need of novice users for detailed and comprehensive directions in order to operate the software with minimal frustration and maximum efficiency.

Instructions are generally provided in one of three modes: (1) a menu format, in which the basic commands and options are displayed on the screen so that the user selects the appropriate command; (2) a series of prompts, which provide the user with choices from which to select the activity or direction to be pursued—repeating, skipping, exiting, moving to the next unit—especially important in programs with branching components; or (3) a turnkey mode, most often occurring in customized software designed for administrative purposes where directions are preformatted to enable the user to operate the program. Whatever mode is utilized for presenting instructions, those directions must be written at a reading level appropriate for the user. One common flaw in educational software occurs when the reading level of instructions is far above the grade level of the subject matter covered in the lesson. An elementary math program, for example, may be preceded by instructions requiring a tenth-grade reading level.

Closely related to the problem of adequate instructions within the software itself is the larger problem of instructions in printed form that accompany software packages, i.e., the problem of documentation. Each software package comes with an operating manual intended to help the user figure out how to load and run the program. Unfortunately, there are too few manuals written in "plain English," and organized systematically for efficient use. Rather, instructions are written in "computerese": they are garbled, jumbled, incomplete, and often incomprehensible, if not entirely omitted. Inadequate instructions for teachers render a program less effective when, for example, reference to important features of the program may be entirely omitted. The teacher may overlook these features or be uncertain about how to utilize them.

A much more universal concern, however, is the lack of support materials comparable to those that accompany textbooks. These include lesson and unit objectives, worksheets, suggestions for supplementary activities, and lists of related print and audiovisual materials.

Teachers have become accustomed to instructional supplements and prefer, if not expect, to find such materials provided by the producers of educational software. Supplementary material, sometimes termed courseware, is more frequently provided by nonprofit educational software producers, such as the Minnesota Educational Computing Consortium (MECC), than by commercial software producers. Because of their marketing experience, textbook publishers expanding into software production are expected soon to be providing more and better courseware with their programs than commercial producers have traditionally done.

An additional functional limitation with which educators are impatient is the often narrow scope of material covered in a given program. Such limited scope necessitates the purchase and use of numerous small programs when one larger, more flexible program would serve equally well for a fraction of the cost. Some educators suggest that instead of separate drill programs for distinct mathematical functions—addition, subtraction, multiplication, division—one larger, flexible program containing drill in several or all of these functions would be preferable. This is undoubtedly more cost-effective and therefore more attractive to school administrators accountable for their budgets. Its feasibility, of course, depends upon the size of the memory in the computer. Many of the micros first purchased by schools may lack the capacity to handle more complex programs. But that limitation, like others we will note, is of short duration as smaller and cheaper microcomputers will contain ever larger memory capacity. The other side of this coin is that some teachers and students undoubtedly prefer to work with clearly identifiable, self-contained units of instructional software. This appeal is no doubt the one that software producers are likely to encourage, since the sale of several separate programs will bring them much greater profits than the sale of a single, multipurpose program. Whether the administrative interest in cost effectiveness or the classroom interest in manageable but more expensive units will prevail remains to be seen.

Most of the functional deficiencies described so far have been largely technical rather than generic or inherent in the nature of the software. One of the more serious flaws in contemporary instructional software—a flaw that borders on being pedagogical—is the limited use made of the vast potential of the hardware. A common criticism is that some programs are so simplistic that they are merely "page turners" or a "workbook on a screen." This criticism, interestingly, is rejected by some software analysts who argue that a "workbook on a screen" is still interactive and therefore much more engaging than a printed workbook could ever be. The validity of the "page turner" criticism depends partly on the sophistication of the workbook pages contained in the program. Generally, the closer the resemblance of the material on the screen to the material in a book, the less interesting it is, and the less it utilizes the potential of the computer.

At a deeper level, software often is criticized for failing to utilize animation or interactive graphics and sound where such components could contribute to a more effective way of presenting certain concepts or information. Animation, for example, could not only enliven but also clarify many physics problems and concepts through demonstration much more effectively than can textbooks. Graphics could bring to life the study of geometry; sound generated to correspond to visual displays could augment the study of music.

As an aid to abstraction, the computer provides a unique and unmatched capacity for developing in users an intuitive grasp of otherwise elusive concepts. Decker Walker relates the experience of the authors of *The Mathematical Experience*, who had spent years trying to get a feel for hypercubes (four-dimensional cubes). Even viewing a film that simulated the visual effect of a hypercube passing through three-dimensional space was only partially enlightening for them. Only after sitting at the controls of the computer and personally manipulating the hypercube did they acquire the long-sought intuitive understanding. "I tried turning the hypercube around, moving it away, bringing it up close, turning it around another way. Suddenly I could *feel* it! The hypercube had leaped into palpable reality as I learned to manipulate it. . . . The active control at the computer consol created a union of kinesthetics and visual thinking which brought the hypercube up to the level of intuitive understanding" Walker, 1983, p. 105; quoting Davis & Heresh, 1981, p. 404].

Once individuals have experienced an abstraction in this mode, they acquire the ability to internalize it, making it accessible for new uses and applications springing from an intuitive level of understanding. This seeming digression on the potential of computers is included not only to emphasize their potential for facilitating much more than basic skills, but also to provide a contrast with the excessively limited graphics and visuals that are too often incorporated into educational programs today.

Graphics and sophisticated visual effects can motivate and augment cognitive and intuitive learning. This is not to say that special effects cannot be overdone. There is, of course, the danger that some producers will replace substance with style—that flashy visuals and sound effects may actually distract from or even subvert the concepts or skills being developed.

A second failure that spans the functional and educational categories of instructional software is the frequent failure to incorporate diagnostic and individualizing components into program design. The efficiency and effectiveness of a given program can be greatly enhanced by segments that determine the student's level of knowledge or skill, automatically branching the student to that portion of the program appropriate for his or her level of readiness. With this provision, slow students could be given the opportunity either to repeat a previous unit or to pursue a similar one until they have reached an acceptable level of mastery; fast students would be branched ahead, skipping those units containing information, concepts, or skill development they have already mastered. Though a few programs such as Radio Shack's *K-8 Math Program* already contain this desirable feature, the flexibility and individualization this program provides are still much more the exception than the rule.

The term "individualization" is usually associated with the object of the process: the student. In a discussion of software, however, it is helpful to expand our understanding and use of the term to refer to the subject doing the individualizing: the teacher. What is desired by many teachers experienced with CAI is software they can modify or individualize for their particular class or a group of students within a class. A spelling or vocabulary program, for example, could be modified by entering the words from a reading assignment or a lesson in another subject area. Or the teacher might modify a lesson by entering words of varying levels of difficulty based on the needs of students in a specific class.

Individualization, we hardly need reminding, has been a concern of educators for several decades. It is therefore only natural that proponents of computerized instruction highlight the capacity of CAI for individualizing the learning process. At present, this capacity is largely undeveloped. What is touted as individualized instruction is, in fact, self-paced instruction—and the two are not synonymous. To make this distinction is not necessarily to denigrate the value of self-paced instruction. One current learning theory actually suggests that the primary difference between achieving and nonachieving students may not be so much in their innate abilities as in the speed with which they learn. Whether or not educators subscribe to this democratic if debatable learning theory, they should have no trouble recognizing the vital role of self-paced instruction in the educational process. Even if current software is more self-paced than individualized, however, we can and should expect more truly individualized instruction from the educational software of the future.

The pacing of material frequently draws criticism from educators who legitimately object to a program in which the computer controls the pace of presentation. A few programs are intended to develop speed in particular skills and therefore are appropriately computer-paced. Most instructional software, however, should allow the user to control the speed of progression so that the pace is comfortable: slow enough for mastery, yet fast enough for challenge. One way of providing for self-pacing is to present material in small segments. Movement between segments occurs only when the user presses a key or gives a designated command. This should, of course, include the option of moving backward as well as forward. If difference in learning speed is a major variance among learners, then software must be designed to accommodate that difference.

Pedagogical Deficiencies

As criticisms of software quality shift in focus from the technical or functional to pedagogical weaknesses, the emphasis concurrently shifts from style to substance. Raising the level of quality by eliminating or minimizing pedagogical deficiencies is generally a complex and difficult undertaking. Instead of adding, eliminating, or modifying relatively minor components of the programs, we are here concerned with altering the academic substance of the software and the application of learning theory in presenting the ideas, information, or skills to be mastered.

Just as improvement of the functional/technical aspects of instructional software runs the gamut from easily corrected problems to more difficult reconstructions, so too is there a range in the simplicity or complexity of the pedagogical problems with today's software. Perhaps the most quickly recognized and least problematic concern is the ability of a program to retain a student's interest. Since user-engagement is likely to be a major selling point, producers are more aware of its importance than they are of other pedagogically critical features.

Though the retention of interest may be less of a problem than some other deficiencies, it does tend to be a special concern with drill-and-practice programs. The elements of reinforcement and pacing are crucial in sustaining a user's interest beyond the first exciting interactions. Graphic and sound reinforcement that involve a long response to a user's input, or that repeat the same response without any variation, soon become tiresome and even irritating. Likewise, extended segments of presentation or explanation with no user activity beyond reading cannot retain a learner's interest much more effectively than a book. Intermittent yet frequent user responses, feedback to those responses, and variety in mode of presentation and reinforcement are all critical elements in sustaining user interest. Of these problems, the absence of immediate, positive reinforcement is among the most critical. Extensive research has provided convincing evidence in support of learning and motivation theory which suggests that both immediate feedback and positive reinforcement measurably improve academic performance. Yet much of the software currently available neglects this important dimension of the learning experience. When the reinforcement is positive, it is too often repetitive in its form, whether visual, auditory or both. To retain its potential for motivation, positive reinforcement must be varied. No matter how "cute" or rewarding a clever response to the right answer, it will lose its effectiveness if repeated without variation.

Positive reinforcement is only appropriate, of course, when the user has given the correct response. The kind of response to a wrong answer is even more important. "Wrong, Dummy," a message actually programed into one producer's software, violates common sense as well as principles of educational psychology. Another counterproductive measure for responding to wrong answers is to provide such a clever response, audio or visual, that the student inserts wrong answers for the sheer entertainment of the machine's response.

A serious flaw in responding to wrong answers is found in programs that simply do not accept or record on the screen any answer but the correct one. With this approach the problem is that learners are tempted to enter a series of answers totally at random until they stumble on the correct one. The "correct" answer in this case reflects no meaningful learning. A more defensible program will respond to a student's wrong answer by providing one or more chances to correct the answer or by giving the correct answer, allowing time for learners to study that answer—or to compare it with their initially incorrect response.

Better still, each incorrect answer should provide the occasion to learn *why* that answer was wrong. Whether learning mathematics or spelling or science, a student who gives a wrong answer has probably failed to understand some concept or principle, unless the answer was the result of carelessness. Good teachers nearly always devote time to "going over" tests at the time the examinations are returned to their students. This exercise enables them to explain why certain answers were right or wrong. Effective instructional software will likewise be structured so that students eventually understand why a given answer is correct or incorrect.

The concern about "right" and "wrong" answers also has a more complex dimension. Students need to confront questions and problems for which there is not necessarily one right answer, but rather several equally acceptable but diverse possibilities, or perhaps even no clear answer. Here we see the beginnings of concern about problem solving and creativity. Regardless of the mode of instruction, a major purpose of problem solving activities is to expand the ways students think about problems. They can be conditioned to expect more than one solution to a given problem, not merely to discover a predetermined solution. This kind of open-ended presentation of problems today is seldom found in educational software. As for creativity, except for the game format so appealing to children of all ages, too few programs either exhibit or foster much creativity. Few programs, for example, require or even encourage students to ask rather than answer questions. Few programs allow students to engage in "what if" kinds of questions, or to follow those questions to a number of possible conclusions.

Our discussion of the pedagogical deficiencies of current educational software, if taken a step further, leads to a still more philosophical concern. Thomas O'Brien raises the issue with conviction in a recent essay: "I have been to dozens of sessions on 'Evaluating Computer Software,' in which the main concern seemed to be that the software should be user-friendly and well documented. If possible, it should also come with laundry lists of behavioral objectives. But there is a more important issue . . . the software should *go somewhere*" [O'Brien, p. 110]. What is meant by the vague term, "going somewhere?" It is a way of focusing our attention on the ends rather than on the means of education—and the end, or aim, of education must be the development of intelligent behavior. O'Brien's description of the "essential abilities for intelligence" includes such skills as the ability to find differences when the similarities are more obvious, and similarities where differences are most readily apparent. Not surprisingly, intelligence is further understood to include creative interpretation and construction of ideas. Education, and more specifically educational software, that "goes somewhere" will facilitate the development of intelligence as we have defined it. That so far neither education nor educational software has been characterized as "going somewhere" very rapidly is no reason to abandon the goal.

Closely related to the substantive issue of the ultimate aim of education, and concomitantly of educational software, is the intriguing distinction O'Brien makes between what he calls static knowledge and dynamic knowledge. As one might surmise, static knowledge goes nowhere, because it is the kind of "single response to a particular, fixed stimulus" that one either has or does not have. Facts that are memorized with no further analysis or application—such as learning by rote memory the capitals of the states or the height of a particular mountain—constitute a major form of static knowledge.

Dynamic knowledge, on the other hand, consists of "a structure of ideas built by action rather than by copying." It is constructed and, if forgotten or lost, unlike static knowledge can be reconstructed. Because it involves thinking processes rather than products, it leads to new knowledge. For all these reasons, dynamic knowledge "goes somewhere."

It is just as unrealistic as it is inappropriate to expect our schools to emphasize dynamic knowledge to the exclusion of static knowledge, but certainly a greater balance between the two is to be desired. Again, the implications for instructional software are obvious: it should further the goals of education. If we want our educational system to foster dynamic knowledge, we should expect educational software to do the same. The potential is there; what remains is to realize that potential.

Careful analysis of the software deficiencies we have discussed leads to some significant conclusions. The most interesting of these pertains to the type of program most susceptible to multiple criticism. Educational software consists of six main types of programs: drill-and-practice; tutorial; simulation; learning game; problem solving; and authoring programs. Of these, drill-and-practice programs attract the most criticism—and not simply because they are the most frequently used and most familiar to classroom users. Recognizing the occasional exception, we must generalize that far too much drill-and-practice software lacks creativity in its conception and fails to stimulate creativity in its users. It lacks variety in mode of presentation. It lacks in quality and variety of positive reinforcement. It seldom begins with or intermittently repeats diagnosis of the user's current level of proficiency, a prerequisite for the branching that constitutes one means of individualizing. It contains little provision for true individualized instruction and little more provision for self-pacing. And it doesn't begin to take advantage of the capability of the hardware. This results in learning experiences essentially similar to those of textbooks, workbooks, and classroom drills. No wonder educators complain most about drill-and-practice software.

The Irony of Drill-and-Practice Criticism

It is curious that teachers should complain because so much instructional software is "merely" drill-and-practice format, as opposed to creative learning games and simulations. Teacher-led classroom drilling exercises are usually tedious for teachers and students alike, as well as notoriously inadequate in meeting the needs and interests of students with vastly different ability and skill levels or rates of learning. That being the case, theoretically teachers should welcome any classroom aid that spares them the tedium of conducting drill-and-practice routines. The literature, in fact, is replete with rhapsodies about the potential for computers to relieve teachers of the tedium and repetition of classroom drills in such areas as spelling, typing, grammar, and arithmetic. Once computers have taken over these odious tasks, most speculate, teachers will be free to spend their time in the more exciting endeavor of developing in students the higher order cognitive skills such as critical thinking, problem solving, and the analysis and synthesis that occupy the upper levels of Bloom's taxonomy.

Current critical reviews of American schooling suggest that many teachers are not equipped to conduct effective learning experiences in the realm of higher order cognitive development. First, they are themselves products of an educational system based on rote learning of information and skills. Lack of experience with and role models for more sophisticated levels of learning constitutes a serious handicap. Second, nothing in most teacher education programs has prepared today's teachers to lead a classroom of students in higher order cognitive development. Instruction and instructors in teacher preparation programs reflect the same lack of exposure to or models for the development of intelligence that afflicts public school instruction. Third, there is little material available from publishers to support higher level intellectual activities, which tends to keep to basic levels the intellectual climate of instruction within the schools. All of these limitations militate against teachers, who are probably not much less comfortable with the "static knowledge" orientation of our current educational system than is the rest of the American public.

Some analysts assume that much of the criticism of drill-and-practice software over other types reflects the deep desire of teachers to escape the drudgery of drill in order to pursue the excitement of intellectual creativity. This assumption, however, ignores the prevailing view of education as a process in which teachers develop in students limited, basic, skills in language and computation, and dispense quantities of information. If this information has recently come to include such socially-oriented topics as health, drug abuse, consumer education, and career education, our view of the nature of education itself has changed little over the centuries.

Only in the rarified atmosphere of educational philosophy and among an almost dying breed of liberal arts devotees do we encounter genuine concern about the aims of education—about the end rather than just the means, about the exposure to dynamic knowledge rather than just static knowledge. And teachers themselves are more likely to share the prevailing view of education held by society than to reflect the concerns of educational philosophers or champion the liberal arts. For that reason, it is hard to be convinced that their criticisms of drill-and-practice software stem from the drive to be released from traditional classroom pursuits in order to engage in the unfamiliar intellectual struggle of promoting disciplined or creative thinking in their students.

The fact is that what most teachers do—and what most have always done—is drill-and-practice. It is unrealistic to expect that once freed of this function they will intuitively, creatively, and competently change their entire style of teaching. To expect that they should even *want* to abandon the activities and teaching styles with which they are so familiar runs contrary to the human tendency to cling to the familiar and comfortable. Even if such adaptations were possible in a relatively short time span, to make those adjustments would imply a radical change in the very nature of education. While some futurists and analysts now predict just such radical change, other social analysts and organizational theorists point skeptically to the inertia of any bureaucracy the size of our educational system. They question the likelihood of any but a gradual, evolutionary change in the nature of American schools.

WHY IS IT A PROBLEM?

That there *is* a problem with the quality of that instructional software currently on the market is one of the new observations about which there is a general consensus. *Why* it is a problem is a more elusive question, the answer to which reflects the different perspectives of those most intimately involved with educational software: those who develop and produce it, and those who use it.

If one asks educators why so many instructional programs are inadequate or unacceptable for the classroom, a typical response would be, "Because programers are not educators, and educators are not programers." What most educators believe is that people trained to write programs usually have no training in learning and motivational theory, no understanding of child development and specifically of intellectual development, and no experience in the classroom that would enable them to create instructionally effective material. It is this lack of knowledge and classroom experience that results in such frustrating software as elementary math programs operated by instructions written at the secondary reading level. It is this same lack of knowledge and classroom experience that results in little or no positive reinforcement, in repetitious positive reinforcement that loses its impact, or in devastating negative reinforcement. It is this same lack of knowledge and classroom experience that accounts for such flaws as designing programs that only accept and record on screen correct answers, or that stop operating when a wrong answer is given, or that include no provision for assuring that students understand why a given answer is wrong. To this extent, when educators identify programers as a factor in the poor quality of the software, they are correct.

Programers and producers, not surprisingly and with some justification, find other reasons for the poor quality of instructional software. They may first return the blame to educators. Teachers don't know what they want, claim many software producers. Do they want drill-and-practice, or simulation, or authoring programs, or what? Do they want to use the computer as an object of instruction—as in computer literacy or computer programing—or as an instructional tool? Given a clear picture of what teachers want, software developers assure us they could then design quality software to meet those desires. In the absence of this information, software producers are reluctant to invest the vast amounts of time and money required to produce quality software, not knowing whether it will be widely and warmly received, or left on the vendors' shelves. (Why they are reluctant to create consumer "needs" where none previously existed, as do so many marketers of new products, is perhaps a question best left unasked.)

Another factor cited by software developers as hindering the production of quality software is the lack of standardization in computer hardware. The profusion of name brands and models of microcomputers—with each model seemingly requiring its own software—militates against even minimal cost-effectiveness in the production of software. Lack of portability, or the capacity of a given program to run on a variety of computer models, means that producers must choose whether to develop their software for a specific model, limiting their market to the owners of that model, or whether to develop software for a variety of computer models or brands, limiting the variety of programs that can be marketed. This latter option is prohibitively expensive and even less desirable than creating software for a market limited to one particular model of computer. Greatly aggravating the problem of diversity in hardware is the fact that microcomputer models, like cars, are continually being "improved," or at least redesigned. Software intended to run on a more primitive model of computer may not run on the new model; or it may run only with the purchase of an additional, and usually expensive, card inserted in the computer to enable it to make the necessary adaptations. These problems are more than excuses on the part of software producers. They are at present legitimate and serious obstacles that have reduced the incentive to invest in the production of more than the simplest of programs.

Yet another factor inhibiting the production of quality instructional software is the relatively small size of the educational market. Although one might think that the large number of schools and classrooms would constitute a sizable clientele, the fact is that the number of homes and businesses far surpasses the number of schools and even the number of classrooms. While the educational market is expected to continue its rapid growth during the next decade, growth in home and business markets will widen an already significant gap. In 1981, one source estimated that of the 20,000 different software programs for computers, only 5 percent were designed for and appropriate to the educational environment [*Electronic Learning*, Nov./Dec. 1981, p. 34]. And while a 1983 National Science Foundation report estimated that there were then 350,000 microcomputers in the classrooms, another source placed the number of home computers in use at 11 million [*Washington Post*, 9/13/83]. Even if the 350,000 micros in the schools are considered to be home computers and subtracted from the 11 million, we have over 10.6 million home computers competing with the schools for the attention and effort of the software producers. And the home market has hardly been dented.

Finally, software producers cite as a major deterrent to the production of quality software the extensive piracy that robs them of a return on their investment. If half of the software in the schools has been illegally copied, as some charge, the problem is obviously a serious one. For each illegally copied and used program, a producer has lost not only a rightful profit, but also the recovery of a portion of the initial investment. Losses of this magnitude cannot be absorbed over any period of time, even in a relatively small market. Such profit losses must be taken seriously by educators, for every pirated program further reduces the quality of available software. The threat of educational software producers to abandon the school market, however, would seem to merit less serious concern. Piracy, we will see in the next chapter, affects all software markets and is hardly confined to the school market. Yet the producers of popular and much-pirated programs for personal and business use (data base managers, word processors, and electronic spread sheets, for example) have never even hinted that they might abandon their enterprise because of piracy. If these developers can live, however unhappily, with diminished profits, one wonders why producers of educational software cannot.

REDEFINING THE QUALITY PROBLEM

Though much of the criticism of the quality of educational software rests upon the prevalence of drill-and-practice programs, this prevalence doesn't necessarily suggest a failure on the part of software producers. Drill-and-practice programs fit the classroom environment and pedagogy. They simply reflect the current status of curriculum, which in turn reflects society's expectations of the schools. Why then the bad press? First, it is generally agreed that drill-and-practice programs do not fully utilize the capacity of the computer, which has the potential to stimulate exciting learning at more complex intellectual levels. Second, reformers who have long been dissatisfied with the limited modes of instruction and lack of intellectual skill development in the precomputer classroom are merely directing those criticisms against the newest kid on the educational block.

If the quality problem with software is not the existence or even the predominance of drill-and-practice programs, is there in fact a problem? If so, what is it? Speakers within the software industry, in assessing the state of the art in educational software, have suggested a variety of answers. Some typical responses are listed below.

(1) The failure is not in the quality of the software; it is the lack of standardization of hardware. If hardware could be standardized, it would stimulate the production of more and better software. The vast number of microcomputers on the market and the constant production of "new, improved" models—which may or may not run the software designed for earlier models—have forced software developers to create programs for the limited market of users owning a particular computer. If they wish to attract users who own other brands or models of computers, software producers must rewrite each instructional program. Rewriting often involves nearly as much effort and expense as writing the initial program.

(2) Teachers don't know what they want. The problem is not quality, but differing opinions about the needs of the classroom and the uses to which instructional software should be put. Whatever a teacher's perception about the kind of software appropriate for the classroom, he or she will be critical of any other type of software produced. The widely differing perceptions of teachers, argue the software producers, necessarily result in a wide variety of criticisms.

(3) Teachers are not adequately familiar with hardware or software. The problem is therefore neither in the software nor in the hardware, but in people. Educators have been slow to learn about and incorporate into the classroom available hardware and software. If they would just learn to use the equipment, educators would be able to locate and use effectively the best software on the market.

These observations on the quality issue are actually assessments of the problems faced by software producers. They should not be confused with assessments of the actual quality of educational software. What each perspective contains is an attempt to redefine the problem. In answering the question "Is there in fact a quality problem and, if so, what is it?" we must construct our own redefinition. The answer is "Yes, there is a software quality problem—but it is transitional."

Regardless of the type of instructional program we consider, the deficiencies described in the earlier portion of this chapter are very real . . . for the moment. Many of them, the reader will recall, fall under the category of functional deficiencies that are relatively easy to remedy. It should be a matter of time before software producers debug their programs of minor operational flaws, correct their spelling and grammar, include more explicit and thorough directions for running their programs, design better ways of handling incorrect responses from users, and improve the visual appearance of the material on the monitor at a given time. Similarly, many educational weaknesses of software can be minimized or overcome with time—and with greater effort. When educators become more actively involved in designing, developing, and testing instructional software, as we expect them to do, we can anticipate improvement in the pedagogical aspects of educational programs. It will come in the form of immediate, frequent, positive reinforcement; more diagnosis and branching to assure maximum self-pacing and individualization; production of more simulation, tutorial, and problem-solving programs; and more effective use of graphics and sound effects to facilitate truly new modes of presenting abstract concepts.

As the current deficiencies in educational software reflect the newness of the enterprise more than the remoteness of improvement, so too do the factors complicating the development of quality software reflect temporary, transitional problems. With time, every teacher will gain experience and some degree of facility with microcomputers and the instructional software being used and marketed for those micros.

Teachers will then have a clearer idea of what they want, what they like, and what they will use their computers for. Once they know this, they can convey their preferences and needs to the software developers, who can then design programs in response to more comprehensive statements of need. This will result in software about which there should be fewer criticisms. Likewise, there is every indication that the lack of standardization is also a temporary, transitional problem. When corporations as influential as both IBM and Apple Computers show serious concern about mutual compatibility, as they recently have done, obstacles to standardization will soon be overcome. As a consequence, software producers will have a vastly expanded market available for any given instructional program in which they choose to invest.

SUMMARY

The quality of instructional software that has so far been available to educators is unquestionably "a problem." Even software producers readily admit the validity of many criticisms of their products. That problem, however, is too quickly summarized as a list of technical and pedagogical deficiencies that, in fact, reflect primarily the inexperience of educators and software producers alike. True, programers without teaching experience can hardly be expected to produce instructionally sound programs, nor can software producers or designers be expected to know what types of programs are wanted or needed in the schools when many educators do not yet know what they want, what works, and why. Nor can educators be expected to have a clear and informed understanding of what they want until they become familiar with the hardware and have experienced enough software to be able to make comparative judgments. But this inexperience should inevitably and relatively soon be remedied by the increasing use of computers in the schools.

What must be kept in mind as educators begin to acquire greater experience and sophistication concerning computer hardware and software, is that much deeper concerns lie just below the surface. What types of programs teachers eventually utilize most will greatly affect how they spend their time in their classrooms. Will their traditional activities of leading classroom drills in knowledge or skill building be replaced by computer drill-and-practice programs? If so, will they have to be retained to acquire the ability to develop higher order cognitive skills in their students? Or will they continue to lead regular classroom drills and use computers for problem solving, development of intellectual creativity, and critical and analytical thinking? The answers to these questions will be formed slowly and probably haphazardly, unless they are confronted with commitment by educators and by society in a disciplined inquiry into the nature and function of modern education.

CHAPTER 3

THE PROBLEM OF COPYRIGHT VIOLATION (PIRACY)

Computers as a technological phenomenon are now over 30 years old. The illegal copying, or pirating, of computer software has emerged as a serious, prevalent problem only within the last five years. Why not earlier? To begin with, until about 1970, software hardly existed as a separate entity; it was included with—and often inside—the hardware purchased by clients of the manufacturers. Then, in 1970, "presumably in response to antitrust pressures" [Milgrim, 1983, p. 158], IBM began selling hardware and software separately.

Illegal copying was neither as feasible nor as tempting in those days when only a few, highly-trained programers had access to a few, complex mainframes for which the software was either built-in or uniquely specific. Computers have been utilized in some of our larger, urban schools for 15 years or more. Here again, they were mainframes, accessible primarily to administrators (often on a time-sharing basis) for scheduling, attendance, and budgeting functions, and to occasional classes of high school students studying computer programing. By 1983, it was estimated that there were 350,000 microcomputers in the schools and 11 million microcomputers in the homes. This new prevalence of microcomputers and easy access to them have made piracy an activity possible at the grassroots level.

As hardware has become dramatically more visible, software too has gained in prominence. Potential users are now generally advised to select or determine the software that will best meet their needs and then purchase the hardware that will run that software. Programs that are relatively simple and narrow in scope are readily available through retailers and through mail order catalogs and computer magazine advertisements. Even copy-protected (or locked) programs become accessible to users who have found commercial or privately developed means of copying programs acquired from friends or from "lending agencies." Possession of these pirated programs enables the pirates to avoid purchasing copies for their own use. Copies can be passed on to family or friends who are then spared the expense of purchasing their own software.

Until recently, hardware was the real profit-making venture of the computer industry. That has been changing as microcomputers have joined telephones and televisions as the technological basics in every home, and as they join textbooks and chalk as the educational basics in every classroom. With hardware installed, sustained interest (and profits) shift to software, for which hardware becomes simply a means to an end. Soon, we are told, "the computer will center on software in much the same sense as the individual motion picture embodied upon film medium is dominant, not the projector or the sound system" [Milgrim, p. 158]. Another analogy drawn by industry observers is that "computer makers will soon mimic camera companies that settle for much lower profit margins on their camera hardware and aim for high margins on their film" ["Missing Computer Software," p. 49]. The implications of this projection offer no great comfort to educators, but they must be considered in our attempts to plan for and shape the future.

IS PIRATING A REAL PROBLEM?

"More than half of the copies of software out there are nonlegal copies," claims Douglas Carlston, president of Broderbund Software Inc. of San Rafael, California. "I'd say that's extremely conservative," responds Brian Lee, vice president of Synapse Software of Richmond, California. After visiting numerous corporations across the nation, Daniel Fylstra, chairman of VisiCorp in San Jose, is convinced that for every copy of the popular *VisiCalc* electronic spreadsheet there is an illegal copy being used. "We still have a viable industry. But it's half the size it should be" [*Wall Street Journal,* Sept. 6, 1983]. These assessments, made during the summer of 1983, reflect the almost unanimous perception of software developers and manufacturers about the extensiveness of copyright violation among users in the field.

Why are developers, producers, and vendors so concerned about copyright violation, more commonly referred to as piracy? The answer, in a word, is "profits." For every illegally reproduced copy in use, producers are deprived not only of their profits, but also of a simple return of their initial investment. That initial investment will vary greatly with the complexity of the program, but a typical estimate for the cost of developing a courseware package is $250,000. Peter Dublin, president of Intentional Education, figures that the basic cost of developing an educational program runs between $20,000 and $40,000 per disk (and as much as $50,000-$100,000 per disk for tools such as even a simple word processing program like the *Bank Street Writer*). This represents merely the cost of *developing* the software and does not take into consideration the expenses of testing, manufacturing, packaging, marketing, overhead, profit, or development of accompanying teachers' guides. Dublin's cost estimate is confirmed by Terry Gilbreth of CBS Publishing Company, who carries the estimate through the additional expenses named above, arriving at a figure of approximately $600,000 for a typical single-grade-level, multidisk program.

With such expenses, software producers have reason to be concerned about the effect of piracy on their investment. According to the *Wall Street Journal*, illegal copying of microcomputer software in 1981 was costing the industry between $12 and $36 million a year, approximately 6-18 percent of total annual sales [*Wall Street Journal*, May 1, 1981].

Perceptions held by individual industry speakers, such as Carlston and Fylstra, are supported by the findings of a recent survey conducted among the software houses producing educational programs for Apple. Of the producers surveyed, 50 percent viewed illegal copying as a moderate or serious threat to profits. That number increased to 75 percent when including only those producers who copy-protect their software [Hoover and Gould, 1982]. Copy-protected disks are designed to prevent users from making additional copies, with the intention that potential users will have to purchase an original disk rather than have access to a working copy. In spite of the extraordinary technological expertise and ingenuity applied to the copy-protection strategies, however, there seems to be comparable expertise and ingenuity applied to defeating those strategies. Brian Lee of Synapse Software estimates that many codes or other protection devices are "cracked" within three to four weeks. And a cracked code or unlocked program is soon followed by the production of a "bit" or "nibble" copier program designed to enable any user to copy the desired program with the "nibbler." Once a program can be copied, it will be, and the producer's profits decline accordingly.

But if profits are the primary source of concern about piracy, and if estimates about the extensiveness of piracy are the subjective projections of those whose profits are at stake, how do we know that such projections are not simply the result of paranoia? An indication of the severity of the problem comes from quarters other than the software producers themselves. The International Council for Computers in Education, which is composed of educators as well as representatives of private enterprise, adopted in June 1983 a Policy Statement on Network and Multiple Machine Software (see Appendix B). This policy statement was developed because an influential group saw the need to protect both the quality of educational software and the profits of those developing that software. While the details of this document will be discussed in greater detail below, reference to it is appropriate here because its very existence implies an issue of such magnitude that educators themselves, who are as a group subject to accusations by producers, are attempting to help control the problem.

The reality of the problem of software piracy is also testified to by recent court cases, though at the time of this writing, the only cases to be brought to the courts have involved systems software—the operating systems built into the hardware. This software is contained not on disks or cassettes but on the microchips inside the computer. It is therefore much more difficult to copy. Enclosed software is of interest primarily to designers and manufacturers, not educators. The issue is therefore tangential to the education-related problems we are considering.[1] Though judicial decisions bestowing copyright privileges on systems software may have implications for the software purchased separately in disk or cassette form, that issue is likewise tangential to the discussion of copying software in the school setting.

---

[1] It should be noted that soon manufacturers are expected to begin to include word processing programs and electronic spreadsheets (the two most popular programs of today's individual and small business buyers) on microchips inside the computer hardware. Perhaps in the future some educational software will be so protected.

We should distinguish between the problem of piracy as it exists and is perceived within the universe of markets (home, school, science, and business) and piracy as it occurs in the educational setting. Whether pirating is more severe in schools than in the other markets is speculative. Whatever the extent of the problem, however, it is serious enough to engage educators and software producers in earnest dialogue in a variety of contexts.

WHY IS PIRACY A PROBLEM?

Why is software piracy in the schools a problem? This may be the only simple question in a lineup of otherwise extremely complex questions regarding current issues and problems in software development. Easy though the answer is, it does contain a four-part response. Software piracy in the schools is a problem because: (1) it is so easy to do; (2) it saves so much money; (3) many teachers are unaware of the copyright law and its applicability to software; and (4) many school districts have not yet developed adequate self-monitoring procedures.

Anyone who has spent an hour or two becoming acquainted with a microcomputer probably knows just how easy it is to duplicate one or more copies from a master disk—especially with dual disk drives. If the particular program is not copy-protected, the procedure is neither complicated nor time consuming. Though much of the educational software is copy-protected (or locked), afficionados and individuals spurred by other motives can find ways to break through whatever technology is devised to protect the program from being copied. There are, furthermore, specific programs called "bit" or "nibble" copy programs with which one can make copies from a master disk. One of Apple's periodicals, *Call—A.P.P.L.E.*, even accepts advertisements for copy programs, though it made the decision to do so only after considerable deliberation. Another duplication aid is the Happy 810 Enhancement device. Its stated function is to increase the speed of an Atari's capacity to read and write data from its memory storage. It also can copy programs. Richard Adams, president of Happy Computing Company of San Jose, compares his device to a photocopier, the function of which is essentially neutral. It can be used legitimately to reproduce uncopyrighted material and to reproduce copyrighted material according to specific guidelines, or it can be used illegally to reproduce material protected by copyright without any regard for fair use guidelines. It is not his Happy 810 Enhancement device that is the culprit, Adams maintains; it is the user who determines whether to employ it for legal or illegal purposes.

The ease with which most programs can be reproduced undoubtedly accounts for much of the extensiveness of pirating activity. Another major factor is the financial savings that accrue to the pirate. Instead of paying anywhere from $30 to $300 or more per program, anyone can buy for a few dollars a blank disk and copy a program onto it. If a school district has acquired multiple units of a particular microcomputer, the natural temptation is to avoid purchasing the equivalent number of multiple copies of a program. With the purchase of one copy and the requisite number of blank diskettes, duplicates can be made to provide one copy for each microcomputer. It is not unusual to hear educators, whether ignorant and well-meaning or sophisticated and resentful of producer prices, justify illegal copying on the grounds of saving the taxpayers' dollars.

A less obvious factor in the extensiveness of software piracy is the lack of awareness on the part of many educators. They may be unaware of copyright law with its provisions for and protection of computer software. Even if they are vaguely aware that copying is likely to be illegal, they may not be aware of the consequences of such illegal reproduction. Nor are most aware of the negative impact of rampant and indiscriminate copying upon software quality. Many teachers are so accustomed to photocopying almost at will that the switch in medium seems a matter of no great import. Increasing numbers of educators have also become accustomed to copying television shows on their videocassette recorders. Computer program copying may seem only a slight technological variation on these already familiar routines.

A final contributing factor to educational software piracy is the lack of self-monitoring by school district personnel. While this factor is related to lack of awareness, it differs in that the focus rests with the administrators to initiate school and district level monitoring. Teachers and other professional staff, of course, should be involved in the design and implementation of such a policy. Its success will depend to a considerable extent upon teacher involvement in continual efforts to enforce the policy among themselves and their students. The existence and implementation of a self-monitoring procedure is the responsibility of district administrators. To design and implement a successful policy, however, all educators in the district should have a reasonably clear idea about the specific language of the copyright law, including provisions for fair use.

WHAT THE LAW SAYS

The most recent copyright law, P.L. 94-553, was adopted by Congress in 1976. The provision pertaining to computers (Section 117) was amended in 1980 by P.L. 96-517. That amendment was anticipated by the framers of the 1976 statute, even though at the time they were unprepared to deal with the complexities of computer copyright and did not want to further retard the passage of a law over 20 years in the making. The original Section 117 provided only that no greater or lesser rights belonged to *owners* of copyrighted works for use in computers and other information systems than to owners of any other copyrighted works. It made no attempt to deal with the possible rights of users of computer software or to address the uniqueness of the technology involved in the creation of computer hardware and software.

The 1980 amendment, itself the product of three years of intensive study by a specially created Congressional commission, consisted of two parts: (1) the addition to the list in Section 101 of the definition of a computer program, and (2) the revision of Section 117, which now specifies the legally acceptable forms of or purposes for copying a computer program, *i.e.*, fair use. Whether or not the amendment enhanced the protection of the owners of copyrighted software or our understanding of user rights is an academic question of more concern to legal scholars than to educators. What should concern educators, because of the limitations on how they may or may not use computers in the schools, are the text of the amendment, the interpretations of that text, and the legal principles for applying the amendment, derived from the 1976 copyright act in its entirety.

Before presenting and analyzing the two components of the 1980 amendment, we must note the potential confusion in any discussion of computer software copyright law resulting from the triple definitions of the term "copy" as used in the copyright act itself. The word "copy" is used in reference to: (1) the verb meaning to reproduce or make duplicate copies from a master copy; (2) the master copy (referred to in Section 117 as a "copy of a computer program"), usually in diskette or cassette form, belonging to the owner who purchases it; and (3) the duplicated or reproduced copy made from the master copy. The context will usually prevent misreadings by the careful reader, but it may be helpful to note that in Section 117, "the copy of a computer program" refers to the originally purchased or owned copy, presumably in disk or cassette form. The present discussion, for clarity and simplicity of expression, will frequently refer to that originally purchased/owned copy as the "master copy" and to a "copied" copy as a "duplicate copy."

What is a computer program? As defined in Section 101 of the Copyright Act, "A 'computer program' is a set of statements or instructions to be used directly or indirectly in a computer in order to bring about a certain result." The application of this definition has proved somewhat problematic in terms of computer programs encoded on the silicon chips embedded within computer hardware. Parties litigating over the "identity" of these silicon chips, which generally contain the operating system for the computer, have argued that the chip is a copy of a computer program (making it copyrightable), or that it is a part of the machinery (making it uncopyrightable). To date, the courts have consistently found the definition of "computer program" to include all of the forms of a program that precede and include the fixing of the program on a disk or cassette, as well as the form fixed on a silicon chip. Details on copyright protection and violation of computer operating systems, however, have little direct bearing on the use of computers in the school setting, and so need not be further discussed here.

In order to understand the title and substance of Section 117, "Limitations on Exclusive Rights: Computer Programs," it is helpful to understand whose exclusive rights are being limited. For that information, we must look to Section 106, "Exclusive Rights in Copyrighted Works." This section delineates the rights of the owner of a copyrighted work, specifically, "the rights to do and to authorize any of the following:

(1) to reproduce the copyrighted work in copies or phonorecords;

(2) to prepare derivative works based upon the copyrighted work;

(3) to distribute copies or phonorecords of the copyrighted work to the public by sale or other transfer of ownership, or by rental, lease, or lending;

(4) in the case of literary, musical, dramatic, and choreographic works, pantomimes, and motion pictures and other audiovisual works, to perform the copyrighted work publicly; and

> (5) in the case of literary, musical, dramatic, and choreographic works, pantomimes, and pictorial, graphic, or sculptural works, including the individual images of a motion picture or other audiovisual work, to display the copyrighted work publicly.

In short, it includes the rights to reproduce, distribute copies to the public, prepare derivative works, and perform or display publicly a copyrighted work belonging solely to the owner of the copyright or to whomever that owner authorizes those rights.

What, then, are the limitations on those exclusive rights of a copyright owner as they pertain to computer software? Section 117 specifies the acceptable reasons for the owner of a computer program to make another copy:

> . . . it is not an infringement for the owner of a copy of a computer program to make or authorize the making of another copy or adaptation of that computer program provided:
>
> (1) that such a new copy or adaptation is created as an essential step in the utilization of the computer program in conjunction with a machine and that it is used in no other manner, or
>
> (2) that such new copy or adaptation is for archival purposes only and that all archival copies are destroyed in the event that continued possession of the computer program should cease to be rightful.
>
> Any exact copies prepared in accordance with the provisions of this section may be leased, sold, or otherwise transferred, along with the copy from which such copies were prepared, only as part of the lease, sale, or other transfer of all rights in the program. Adaptations so prepared may be transferred only with the authorization of the copyright owner.

At first glance, this provision may appear perfectly simple and straightforward. In fact, most readers probably wonder why the framers of this amendment felt it necessary to protect the obviously legitimate function of entering or loading a program into a computer ("an essential step in the utilization of the computer program in conjunction with a machine"), and why, furthermore, that process should constitute copying at all. Some insight can be gained by reading *Final Report of the National Commission on New Technological Uses of Copyrighted Works*, hereafter referred to as the CONTU Report. The product of three years of study by a Congressionally appointed commission, the 1978 CONTU Report has had significant impact on national policy. The amendment itself is nearly identical to the statement recommended by CONTU. The CONTU Report has also influenced judicial rulings pertaining to the copyrightability of computer programs, where the impact is apparent in the frequent citations from the Commission's report.

Why did the Commission define loading a program into a computer as an act of copying, and why should that seemingly innocuous—even essential—act require statutory protection? The Report contains this explanation:

> The text of the new copyright law [1976] makes it clear that the placement of a copyrighted work into a computer—or, in the jargon of the trade, the "inputting" of it—is the preparation of a copy. This may be ascertained by reading together the definitions of *copies* and *fixed* found in section 101. In pertinent part, they read as follows:
> "Copies" are material objects . . . in which a work is fixed. . . .
> A work is "fixed" . . . when its embodiment in a copy . . . is sufficiently permanent or stable to permit it to be perceived, reproduced, or otherwise communicated for a period of more than transitory duration.
> Because works in computer storage may be repeatedly reproduced, they are fixed and, therefore, are copies. [p.22]

Knowing why, or accepting the legal assertion that the entry of a program into a computer's memory involves a form of copying, may still leave the reader wondering what potential problems could arise to necessitate protection of this seemingly simple, straightforward activity, technically defined as copying. This activity, however, is only simple and straightforward when it involves an individual owner of a copy of a program using a single, self-contained machine such as a microcomputer. There are, however, many other variations of this activity, especially within the school environment. These variations are not explicitly covered by Section 117. They include networking between computers within a school or school system; using a single disk to boot up sequentially a series of separate computers; making and keeping of archival copies by school libraries; and designating the school district as owner of the software because the district has purchased that software. Each of these situations raises its own issues. Networking raises the questions of defining "a machine" and of the legality of simultaneous users of a single copy of a program. Sequentially booting up several machines with one disk also raises the question of applying "the utilization of the computer program in conjunction with a machine." Making, using, and keeping archival copies in school libraries raises such questions as the legality of making another back-up copy from the archival copy in the event that a student destroys the borrowed copy. And finally, a school district as the owner of computer software may raise questions about single versus collective owners, as well as the rights of school districts licensing or leasing their software.

HOW THE LAW IS INTERPRETED

That a law written in black and white should be subject to several interpretations should come as a surprise to no one in the field of education. Few legal questions, especially in the early phases of their appearance as issues, draw unanimity of response from legal experts. The copyright issues pertaining to computer programs are no exception. Most of those questions arise from attempts to apply the law to various uses of computer software.

Before a law can be applied, it must be interpreted, and educators must be aware of two very different interpretations of Section 117. One interpretation, engagingly and cogently presented by Daniel Brooks in his essay included in Appendix A, is built on the reading of Section 117 as a provision to control the proliferation of *users*, not the proliferation of *copies*. Under this interpretation, the owner of a master copy of a computer program can make any number of duplicate copies for personal use. Those copies must be retained *solely* for personal use and are not to be distributed to others—unless those copies are accompanied by the master copy. Proponents of the alternate interpretation hold that Section 117 very explicitly prohibits the proliferation of copies beyond the one back-up or archival copy allowed. In our attempt to understand the rationale on which each interpretation is based, we will begin to see the shadows of the legal principles for applying the copyright law that we will later examine in detail.

"Proliferation of Users, Not Copies"

How can Section 117 be construed to allow the proliferation or copying of multiple copies of a computer program? It does state, after all, that the owner of a copy of a computer program may only make "another copy" (singular) or "adaptation" (also singular). Yet adherents of the "proliferation of users" interpretation maintain that a person in legitimate possession of a master copy may make as many duplicate copies as he wishes, *provided* that he abides by the restriction that the transferral of the duplicated copies include transferral of the master copy as well. In other words, an individual may make ten back-up copies for personal archives, but may not distribute those copies to other individuals without giving up possession of the originally owned copy. Since Section 117 provides for the making of "another copy or adaptation" (not for "other copies and adaptations"), and since the singular form of the terms is used not just once but three times, does it not seem likely that the authors of that provision intended it to allow the making of only *one* archival copy? Probably so, as we will see later.

There are, however, several considerations that serve to justify the "proliferation of users" interpretation. The first one is based on the second to last sentence of Section 117, which reads: "Any exact *copies* prepared in accordance with the provisions of this section may be leased, sold, or otherwise transferred, along with the copy from which such copies were prepared" [emphasis added]. This sentence has been construed as permitting the proliferation of copies while restricting the proliferation of users. It does, after all, refer to "copies" in the plural form. The difficulty with the reading is that the plural use of "copies" is followed by the qualification "*prepared in accordance with the provisions of this section*." That, of course, refers back to the preceding statements, all three of which specify the making of a singular "copy or adaptation." An alternate and equally defensible reading of this sentence, then, would construe the plural form of "copies" as referring to the collective making of copies by individuals who have each abided by the restrictions of making one archival copy. More succinctly, "copies" in this sentence may well refer to several individuals who make single copies, rather than to one individual who makes several copies. In the light of this alternate construction of the provision in question, the first rationale for the "proliferation of users" interpretation must be considered arguable at best.

A more convincing rationale exists, however, for interpreting the Copyright Act as permitting an individual to make multiple copies from a master copy he owns, provided that those copies are not distributed to others without being accompanied by the master copy. That rationale is grounded in an understanding of the function of copyright protection and of the fair use concept that attempts to protect certain potential users of copyrighted material. Specifically, copyright law is designed to protect the financial interests of creative individuals. One of the basic tests for determining copyright infringement, then, is the "market effect" test. A basic question in applying that test becomes: Has the copyright owner been deprived of income? Even the fair use provision, Section 107, which was written to protect educational and media-related uses of copyrighted works, includes several factors pertaining to the commercial aspects of the copyright problem. Two of the four factors contained in Section 107 make explicit reference to the financial aspects of copying copyrighted works, and the other two factors are indirectly related to this same concern. In short, given the purpose of the copyright law, the market effect test will necessarily be a central—though not necessarily the single—test in resolving any question of copyright infringement. In this light, it becomes reasonable to interpret the copyright law as allowing an individual who owns a copy of a computer program to make as many copies of that program as he or she wishes, as long as those copies are retained *only* for personal use. The existence of these duplicate copies in no way deprives the copyright owner of any profits, nor does it affect the potential market for or the market value of the copyrighted work. Proponents of this construction of the law therefore argue that there is no copyright infringement when a person makes a number of back-up or archival copies of computer programs, as long as that person never distributes those copies to others while retaining the master copy.

Whether a judge or jury would find this argument convincing might depend upon their inclination toward a strict construction of Section 117, or a more permissive construction of Section 117 in the context of the copyright law in its entirety. And while the problem may be largely academic or hypothetical in terms of a given individual unobtrusively making a couple of extra back-up copies in the privacy of his home, it could become more pragmatic and significant when the owner is a school district. However, even the legal experts subscribing to the more liberal construction of the law do not suggest that a school can legally buy one copy of a computer program and make multiple copies for simultaneous use by students.

The other rationale supporting the "proliferation of users" interpretation is the fair use concept embodied in Section 107. To treat here the complexity of Section 107 and its centrality in understanding the applications of copyright law to the educational setting would involve too great a digression. A brief description of its relevance, however, is necessary if reference to fair use is to be at all meaningful.

Though there are several ways of "unpacking" Section 107, it is possible to view the fair use provision as, among other things, an additional reinforcement of the market effect test. This view stems from the four factors included in Section 107 for determining fair use. Of those four factors, two explicitly refer to the commercial dimension of copying copyrighted material: whether the copying is for nonprofit, educational use or for commercial use, and whether the copying affects the potential market of the copyrighted work. The other two implicitly support protection of the financial interests of copyright owners: the nature of the copyrighted work and the proportion of the amount copied in relation to the entire work. In short, since fair use is a concept developed with nonprofit educational institutions in mind, and since it nevertheless is circumscribed by boundaries involving the commercial aspects of copying, it can be interpreted as permitting a proliferation of copies—as long as that proliferation in no way adversely affects the financial interests of the copyright owner.

"Single, Not Multiple, Copies"

In spite of a solidly based rationale for the "proliferation of users" interpretation of Section 117, that interpretation is not accepted by all specialists in copyright law. Several of the attorneys who served as commissioners or staff members of CONTU,[2] when questioned about the phrasing of Section 117, confirmed the deliberateness with which the commissioners selected the singular rather than the plural form of the words "copy or adaptation." These individuals were also quick to confirm that the commissioners intended the singular form to be understood literally. The law as enacted was not intended to permit

---

[2] Melville Nimmer, vice-chairman of the Commission; Arthur Levine, executive director of the Commission staff; and Michael Keplinger, assistant executive director and senior attorney of the Commission staff.

reproduction of multiple copies of a computer program in any context or by any individual, they contend.

While such statements represent admittedly subjective interpretations of intent, we might anticipate that a court would weigh seriously these statements along with the CONTU Report itself. For one thing, legislative history is frequently given consideration by the courts when there is need to interpret or apply statutory law to a specific problem. The CONTU Report, containing the recommendation for an amendment that was nearly identical to Section 117 as enacted by Congress, provides a context for understanding that section and the intent of those who hammered it out. The weight accorded the CONTU deliberations can further be ascertained from the fact that all of the eight judicial decisions pertaining to the copyrightability of operating systems (software embedded in silicon chips inside the computer) followed the reasoning of the report. Specifically, the Commission held that a computer program is defined from the earliest flow chart phase, through development of source and object codes, and finally even including encoding onto silicon chips. Court decisions to date reflect this same position, and several of them specifically cite the CONTU Report. It seems likely, therefore, that the perspective of the Commission would be given equally serious consideration by a court deciding a case involving the construction of Section 117.

SUMMARY

Applying Section 117 of the Copyright Act to the use of instructional software seems easy at first—deceptively so. It is simple as long as a teacher or student uses a copy of a computer program as any law abiding individual outside the school setting would use it. The typical "law abiding" person loads his or her master copy of the program into a microcomputer and runs it. Although by definition in the Copyright Act, this use of the computer program constitutes "copying," it is one form of copying that is legally acceptable and protected. The only other form of copying that does not constitute copyright infringement is the making, by the owner of a master copy, of an archival or back-up copy. From this point, application of Section 117 becomes more problematic.

At issue is whether the owner of a master copy may make *only* one back-up copy for archival purposes, or whether the owner of a master copy may make several duplicate copies for archival purposes. Some legal scholars construe Section 117 strictly, advising users to limit themselves to making one and only one archival copy. Other legal scholars construe Section 117 more liberally, based on legal principles derived from the nature and function of the copyright law as a whole. They interpret the law as permitting users to make multiple back-up copies, as long as those copies are retained by the owner and kept at all times with the master copy.

Interesting though this debate is, it is not the most urgent or pressing of the issues facing educators today who are concerned about the legal use of computer software in their schools. Section 117 provides little if any assistance in analyzing those complex and urgent problems. There is, fortunately, an additional perspective available from which to assess the potential legality or illegality of the problematic uses of educational software. That perspective is gained with an understanding of the legal principles derived from years of copyright litigation and legal analysis—and it is discussed in the next chapter.

CHAPTER 4
LEGAL PRINCIPLES FOR APPLYING COPYRIGHT LAW TO SOFTWARE USE IN THE SCHOOLS

The copyright law as it pertains to copies of computer programs, we learned in the preceding chapter, explicitly prohibits the making of duplicate copies of an owned copy of a computer program for distribution to or use by others. Interpretations vary, we also learned, as to the rights of the owner of a master copy to make more than one archival copy for personal use. But the legal technicalities of that particular issue seem rather academic and the problem hypothetical in comparison to the issues raised by the use of computers and computer software in schools. In the educational setting, there are several perplexing problems frequently raised.

The development and use of a variety of networks—a phenomenon that raises questions of defining "a machine"—is no small concern when applying Section 117 to the use of a computer program in a network. Another issue raised by educators involves the legality of sequentially booting up a number of microcomputers in a classroom or lab with only one copy (disk or cassette) of a program. There is also the question of distinguishing between simultaneous multiple users and sequential multiple users of a single copy of a computer program. And there are questions pertaining to the making and using of copies in the context of a school or other public library. Since Section 117 does not provide a clear and simple criterion for determining the legality of these more complex questions, we must turn to the legal principles that have been developed during the history of copyright law and to the legal thinking that is currently being applied to recent technological developments.

FIVE CONSIDERATIONS

There are several legal principles or tests which can be applied to issues facing educators concerned about legally acceptable uses of their computer software. Of the five principles listed below, the first has already been discussed in some detail; the other four require explanation. Those five principles or tests are as follows:

1. **Market effect test:** Will the questioned use of the software deprive the copyright owner of income? Will the practice in question reduce the sale of copies by the number of students simultaneously accessing and using one copy?
2. **Intended use test:** For what purpose was the software designed? Was it intended for use in a single microcomputer by a single user, or for use in a network by simultaneous multiple users?
3. **Fair use principle:** Section 107 lists four factors for determining fair use of copyrighted material in an educational setting. Which, if any, of those four factors sheds light on the questioned use of the software?
4. **Simultaneous versus sequential users:** Whether this is a problem to be resolved or a principle for resolving other problems is itself debatable. Most copyright specialists find the distinction significant, holding that simultaneous multiple users are potentially infringing upon copyright protections, and that sequential multiple users are within legally acceptable bounds.
5. **Licensing agreements:** Is the purchased software accompanied by a licensing agreement? If so, what restrictions does the license impose upon the owner/user?

The Market Effect Test

The function of copyright law to protect the financial interests of copyright owners, we have seen, inevitably necessitates some reliance upon the market effect test. Several questions or guidelines are helpful to the software user in applying this test. One is to ask: Am I depriving the copyright owner of income? That is, am I making my copy of the computer program accessible to others with the result of depriving the copyright owner of profits from program sales? Or, at the school district level, are we making one copy of a computer program accessible to students in such a way that we save ourselves the expense of purchasing the requisite number of additional copies needed to service those students? In either case, the owner of the copyright for that program is being deprived of profits from the sale of copies equivalent to the number duplicated or the number of students simultaneously using that program.

A closely related guideline is the golden rule for computer users, attributed to Joseph McDonald: "Take not from others to such an extent and in such a manner that you would be resentful if they so took from you." Applying this test requires only that the user imagine being the owner of the copyrighted program in question, and asking how he or she would feel about the contemplated copying or use of that program. If you, as copyright owner, would be upset by a specific mode of using your program in your school, then you as an educator should probably refrain from such use.

The Intended Use Test

The second test or legal principle for applying copyright law to the use of computer software in the schools involves identifying and abiding by the intended use of the software. This test is especially helpful in resolving questions about using software in a network of microcomputers. Educators applying this principle should ask themselves whether the program was designed, and therefore intended, for use in a network. If so, using it in a network seems unlikely to constitute infringement of copyright. Should the program have been designed for use by a single user operating a self-contained microcomputer, then making it accessible to several users through a networking arrangement seems a likely violation of copyright law. It is worth noting that the intended use test is not unrelated to the market effect test; if a program is developed and produced with the intention of its being used in a network, such use does not deprive the copyright owner of income, nor would that owner be resentful that the program is being used as intended.

The Fair Use Concept

Fair use, a concept embodied in Section 107, also reflects the commercial concerns that constitute the *raison d'etre* for the rest of the Copyright Act—even though it is intended to balance the interests of copyright owners with the needs of others for access to copyrighted material. Fair use of copyrighted material is not limited in scope to educators. Its purpose is to protect or support a number of functions that rely on access to entire works or excerpts from creative works. Teaching and research, media reporting, and criticism are foremost among activities cited for their dependence upon access to and use of copyrighted works. Because of the centrality of Section 107 to any understanding of copyright as it applies to educational settings and personnel, the text of that section is included in its entirety below.

> Notwithstanding the provisions of Section 106, the fair use of a copyrighted work, including such use by reproduction in copies or phonorecords or by any other means specified by that section, for purposes such as criticism, comment, news reporting, teaching (including multiple copies for classroom use), scholarship, or research, is not an infringement of copyright. In determining whether the use made of a work in any particular case is a fair use the factors to be considered shall include—
>
> (1) the purpose and character of the use, including whether such use is of a commercial nature or is for nonprofit educational purposes;
>
> (2) the nature of the copyrighted work;
>
> (3) the amount and substantiality of the portion used in relation to the copyrighted work as a whole; and
>
> (4) the effect of the use on the potential market for or value of the copyrighted work.

A quick glance at the four criteria for determining fair use reveals that some criteria are more directly enlightening than others as we attempt to apply them to the copying of instructional software. The first criterion, pertaining to the purpose and character of the use, includes specific mention of the distinction between commercial or nonprofit educational use. Ideally, and perhaps realistically as well, teachers would most likely use copied programs for educational purposes rather than for commercial profit. But it is dangerous for educators to assume fair use simply because their making multiple copies from a master copy of a computer program results in no profits for them or for the school district. They should not jump to the conclusion that their copying will be considered a fair use just because no commercial benefit was gained from their copying or using illegally copied programs. Lack of monetary gain and "good intentions" are insufficient to substantiate the defense of fair use. Another way of emphasizing this same conclusion is to point out that purely educational use of illegally copied programs has not sheltered anyone from charges of copyright infringement.

The second criterion pertains to the nature of the copyrighted work. Discussion of this factor in the Senate committee report distinguished between informational and creative material. Copying news articles from a daily press, we learn, would be judged more leniently than copying the complete orchestral score of a musical composition or a consumable article designed for classroom use, such as a workbook page. Materials prepared for distribution to the general public would be inherently less problematic than materials prepared for classroom use—a distinction not unrelated, again, to the market effect criterion. Obviously, someone who creates materials to be sold for classroom instruction will lose profits by the photocopying of those materials. On the other hand, a newspaper reporter, working for a salary, compiles and writes information that may well be accessible in other sources, and that will generally have interest only for a limited time. In either event, there is little if any financial loss to the reporter or to the publisher when an individual or educator photocopies what is undoubtedly a small portion of the news or editorial analysis contained in a newspaper, magazine, or periodical. Applying this criterion to computer software provides little encouragement to educators, since instructional software, by definition, is designed for educational purposes. Any copying of a program designed for the classroom would be, then, less rather than more defensible than copying a program designed for general, noneducational purposes (were copying of *any* programs defensible). Again we can see the connection with market effect and intended use of tests.

Where the fair use concept becomes at once more complex and more straightforward is with the third criterion: "the amount and substantiality of the portion used in relation to the copyrighted work as a whole." The intent here, as described in the Senate report, was to allow teachers to copy excerpts from larger works as representative or illustrative of the works of their authors. The allowable quantity of copyable material depends less upon number of lines or pages than on its proportion to the quantity of the work from which the material is taken. Five pages copied from an eight-page work are not comparable to five pages copied from a 500-page work. Illustrating or representing the work of an author is the other consideration, which is also distinguished from embodying the essence of that work. This consideration could qualify a judgment otherwise based on the amount or proportion of the work copied, theoretically rendering the reproduction of even five pages from a 500-page work susceptible to a verdict of infringement, if those five pages somehow captured the very essence of the work itself.

As applied to software, the practical effect of this third criterion is to reinforce the prohibition against copying computer programs for classroom use. Since a computer program as it exists in diskette or cassette form would not be functional in fragments, even if it were possible to copy only fragments, the typical nonprograming educator has neither the ability nor the need to try to copy a portion of an instructional program. (The display to a programing class of a portion of a program code is another matter, dealt with in the paper by Daniel Brooks.) If motivated to copy at all, an educator is most likely to want or need to copy the entire computer program, and that, clearly, is not within the scope of this criterion of fair use.

The fourth and last criterion, however, is not only the most decisively enlightening when applied to computer software, but it is also the basic principle to which the preceding three criteria are directed. "[T]he effect . . . upon the potential market for or value of the copyrighted work" is in essence the ultimate concern underlying the prohibition of copying for commercial rather than for nonprofit educational purposes, of copying creative works as opposed to informational works, and of copying the major portion of a work as opposed to a small excerpt. The market effect, we can see, is so fundamental a concern that all the other fair use considerations must be understood in relationship to it.

The Senate report illuminates the parameters intended by Congress in applying the market effect test to classroom use of copyrighted material. Among other things, photocopying is permissible to the extent that it augments purchased material rather than replaces the use of material that would otherwise have been purchased. Furthermore, the report explains, "[f]air use is essentially supplementary by nature, and classroom copying that exceeds legitimate teaching aims such as filling in missing information or bringing a subject up to date would go beyond the proper bounds of fair use." By this standard, the illegality of copying complete computer programs should be obvious. And it constitutes merely a more specific application of the general criterion itself: what is the effect of copying upon the potential market for the copyrighted work? To copy a program for the use of someone else who would otherwise have had to purchase that program—or in the case of schools, to make several copies of programs in lieu of purchasing them—has the unquestioned effect of reducing the number of potential sales by the number of copies made or by the number of students simultaneously accessing the program. That effect upon the market renders such copying outside the scope of fair use and therefore illegal, regardless of the purpose or motive.

These four criteria, standing alone, provide only general hints as to what constitutes fair use. Fortunately, they were augmented with discussion contained in the report of the Senate committee, which clarifies the intent of the legislators who passed the bill. Additional parameters, developed by educators, writers, and publishers, were also incorporated in the report accompanying the House version of the bill. Known as "Guidelines for Classroom Copying in Not-for-Profit Educational Institutions," those guidelines were developed to establish minimum standards of educational fair use. Though they pertain to printed media, some attorneys specializing in copyright law believe that these guidelines serve at least a limited function in furthering our understanding of the concept of fair use as it applies to educational software.

More relevant than the guidelines applicable to reproduction of printed materials for classroom use are the "Guidelines for Off-Air Recording of Broadcast Programming for Educational Purposes." These guidelines, too, are the product of extended negotiation among educators, media representatives, and authors and artists. Each of the three documents—the Senate report elaborating on the four criteria for fair use, the print media guidelines contained in the House report, and the off-air recording guidelines—will be discussed below.

Most discussions of fair use as applied to reproduction of copyrighted material for the classroom include reference to the "Guidelines for Classroom Copying in Not-for-Profit Educational Institutions." These guidelines, drawn up by educators, authors and publishers, were included in the report accompanying the House version of the bill that eventually became the Copyright Act. The complete text of these guidelines is found in Appendix C. They distinguish first of all between the making of single copies by teachers for use in their research or preparation for classroom teaching and the making of multiple copies for use by students. Guidelines for (or restrictions on) the former are reasonably liberal, even from an educator's perspective. Guidelines and restrictions regarding multiple copies for classroom use, on the other hand, are undoubtedly perceived as more conservative from an educator's perspective than from that of a publisher. While familiarity with these guidelines can provide educators with insight into the application of fair use principles, their *direct* relevance to the copying of computer software is limited because they were designed for the print media. The brevity test, especially, sheds little light on the problem of reproducing educational software, given the unlikely occurrence of educators attempting to copy only portions of an educational computer program. The spontaneity and cumulative effect tests are not signficantly more enlightening. Given the Section 117 limitation of making "a copy or adaptation" for archival purposes or for utilization in a machine, the spontaneously illegal copying of a computer program is no more justifiable than the premeditated illegal copying of that program. The cumulative effect test might simply render a teacher liable to more severe penalty for repeated use of illegally copied software or the repeated illegal copying.

The most pertinent guideline is found in Section III(C), which reads: "Copying shall not: (a) substitute for the purchase of books, publishers' reprints or periodicals." Certainly, the reproduction of disks or cassettes for student use in the school environment can be viewed as comparable to the proscribed substitution for purchasing textbooks or other published instructional materials. We may reasonably conclude, then, that if legal experts find the Guidelines for Classroom Copying (of print media) helpful in providing a general understanding of the fair use concept, these guidelines serve only to reinforce the general restrictions of the fair use provision, rather than expand them to permit the making of multiple copies for any reason.

Because computer software is technologically more similar to audio-visual media than to print media, some copyright specialists regard the recent "Guidelines for Off-Air Recording of Broadcast Programming for Educational Purposes" as having greater relevance for understanding the copyright law as it regulates the use and defines abuse of computer software. These guidelines were painfully hammered out among representatives from educational organizations, copyright proprietors, creative guilds, and unions over a period of about two years. Completed in the summer of 1981, the off-air recording guidelines were later ratified by the House Subcommittee on the Courts, Civil Liberties, and the Administration of Justice. Though they do not have the legal status of legislation, they are understood as part of the legislative and social context of the 1976 Copyright Act. As such, they are likely to withstand close scrutiny in the courts (see Appendix D).

Simultaneous versus Sequential Users

The fourth legal principle for applying copyright law to the use of computer software in an educational setting focuses on the distinction between simultaneous and sequential users. That principle, affirmed by nearly all computer copyright specialists, allows for sequential but not for simultaneous multiple users of a given computer program. An immediate response of a lay reader might be to ask why sequential multiple use of a master disk does not constitute the proscribed "proliferation of users." The basis for this distinction is found in the right of any owners of a copy of a computer program to do with that program what they wish, as long as they are not making multiple copies of it. The owner may, for example, allow another person to use the program in the owner's computer; the owner may allow another person to borrow that program; or the owner may use his own program in someone else's computer. All of theses rights pertain only if the program was not accompanied by a license prohibiting such uses. Because the owner of a master copy of a computer program may loan that copy to any number of individuals, and the loans must necessarily be sequential, it is generally accepted among copyright specialists that owner-loaners who facilitate sequential multiple users are not likely to be susceptible to charges of infringement (barring their knowing complicity in illegal uses by the borrowers of their master copies).

Simultaneous multiple users, on the other hand, certainly pose the probability of copyright violation, for the very reason that in order for a copy of a program to be accessible to simultaneous multiple users, multiple copies of the master copy must be made. That they are not necessarily made in tangible form on cassette or diskette does not mean the copies have not been made. (Keep in mind the CONTU Report's understanding of "copy" as including all forms of a program.) Transferring copies from a master copy into the memories of networked microcomputers may well be considered "copying" as defined in the copyright law. Making a master copy of a computer program (designed for a single user) accessible to simultaneous multiple users is also much more likely to fail the market effect test than is the accessing by sequential users. Ten users wanting to use a given program simultaneously have two choices: purchasing ten copies of the program or accessing it via a network. The latter would then deprive the owner of the copyrighted program of the profits from the sale of nine copies. In short, while both sequential and simultaneous users of a particular copy of a computer program constitute proliferation of use, sequential users are more likely to be within the legal boundaries of the copyright law; simultaneous users most likely are not within those boundaries.

Licensing Agreements

The fifth and last test for determining legally acceptable uses of computer software in the schools involves identifying and abiding by any restrictions contained in the lease that often accompanies a master copy of a computer program. Many software producers automatically include a contract or license agreement, written into the manual or other material accompanying the disk or cassette. That license becomes effective from the moment the purchaser opens the package containing the software. While the exact wording of the entire license will vary from one company to another, a typical restriction reads as follows: "Lawful users of this program are hereby licensed only to read the program from its medium into memory of a computer for the purpose of executing this program. Copying, duplicating, selling or otherwise distributing this product is hereby expressly forbidden." Samples of other license agreements are included in Appendix F for the purpose of alerting readers to the nature and importance of these licenses. What owners and users must remember is that program licenses constitute legal documents. If they are more stringent than federal copyright law, they must nevertheless be strictly adhered to if users want to avoid prosecution for violating the license to which they agreed through the act of purchasing the program covered by that license.

USING SOFTWARE IN THE SCHOOLS LEGALLY

Because there have been no court cases to date ruling on the legality of specific uses of software in the schools, and due to the complexities of both the technology and the law involved in using computers in the schools, it is unrealistic to expect many definitive answers to questions about legal and illegal uses of software in an educational setting. The absence of definitive answers, however, does not mean there are no answers. It does mean that educators will have to exercise their own judgments on the basis of authoritative opinions concerning a number of their most pressing questions. The problematic situations mentioned only briefly at the beginning of this chapter will be presented here in more detail, and the legal principles discussed above will be applied to those situations.

One question asked by educators out of genuine interest or with a touch of sauciness—depending upon their sophistication with computers—is: "What if I take the school's one disk, boot it into one student's microcomputer, remove it, and successively boot it into ten more micros in my classroom? I'm not duplicating extra disks, so where's the problem?" The problem is, unfortunately, that the proscribed making of more than one archival copy from a master copy is not limted to copies in disk or other tangible form. As we have seen, the copyright law defines as "copy" any copy "from which the work can be . . . reproduced, or otherwise communicated, either directly or with the aid of a machine or device." Even if it were argued that this use of the disk constituted the legally acceptable copying "as an essential step in the utilization of the computer program in conjunction with a machine" (Section 117), which might be legitimately argued, a prosecutor could respond that this essential step is being taken in conjunction with *several* machines, not *a* machine. The market effect test further renders this action highly dubious because it deprives the copyright owners of income. What software producer would not be resentful of the loss of profits accruing from the sequential loading and then simultaneous use by ten students of one copy of that producer's program? If the program seems intended for operation by one user rather than several, this simultaneous use by ten students at ten microcomputers of one copy of a program is likely to fail the intended use test. And even if the program is sequentially booted into several different computers, it is being run simultaneously by several users, thereby failing the simultaneous users test. In short, sequential booting up of several computers with one disk or cassette appears to violate all four aspects of the copyright-based legal principles for using software in the schools. And if the program is accompanied by a license, the sequential booting of one disk into multiple units of microcomputers undoubtedly violates the common license provision prescribing use in just one machine.

The other question most frequently asked by educators is: "What about networking? May we load a copy of a program into the hard drive of a computer to which multiple units of microcomputers are connected in a network arrangement? We're not multiplying the number of copies, after all." Different though this situation seems from the previous one of sequentially booting up a series of unconnected microcomputers, the effect of such use is much the same, and the application of legal principles leads to the same conclusions. There are, to be sure, a variety of technically different network systems. These run the gamut from mainframes connected to dumb terminals (without their own central processing units), microcomputers connected to mainframes (still infrequent in the schools), and microcomputers connected to a centralized microcomputer adapted with a hard drive. Any one or more of these network systems might be located in a lab, in a classroom, throughout a school, or perhaps even throughout a school district.

Though some network variations raise the issue of defining "a machine," and "a machine" might well be defined either in terms of the hardware or the software, these considerations involve highly technical analyses that have yet to be fully developed. Furthermore, even if the technical and consequently the legal aspects were more clearly established, any plaintiff pressing charges of infringement would undoubtedly insist on application of the appropriate legal principles as well. Applying these legal principles to the problem of networking, we find the market effect and intended use tests, taken together, especially helpful. If the program was designed for use in a network system, it seems reasonable to assume that using it as it was intended should pose few foreseeable problems. It seems equally reasonable to assume that the copyright owner is not being deprived of income by such use. If, however, the program was not designed to be used in a network (and most instructional programs to date are not so designed), such use is risky indeed. The simultaneous users test by itself is not helpful here because of unresolved questions about the definition of "a machine." But simultaneous users inescapably lead one to the market effect and intended use tests as applied above.

Even fair use provides little comfort to educators looking for justification for using one copy of a program in a networking system. The market effect test—one of four factors in the fair use concept—has already been discussed and obviously calls most networking into question. The "nature of the work" factor renders such use even more questionable, since the copying is of a work intended for the classroom. It neither is supplementary, nor makes information accessible that is not readily available on the market for instructional purposes. The amount or substantiality of the portion copied further renders networking questionable. The entire program must be "copied" in order for students at networked stations to use it. The best—and perhaps the only—means of "legalizing" the networking of a program otherwise designed for use by a single user in a single machine is to obtain a license agreement from the copyright owner permitting its use in a network system. That license, in effect, obtains the copyright owner's permission for the desired use. All of the specific prohibitions contained in the coypright law are applicable only *absent* authorization of the copyright owner.

ADDITIONAL CONSIDERATIONS

Owner/user distinction. It should be noted that Section 117 refers to the rights of the "owner" of a copy of a program to make the archival copy and to make the copy necessary for utilization in the machine. The CONTU Report recommended that such rights accrue to "the rightful possessor," but Congress was concerned to exclude borrowers and lessees of software from the ranks of those who can legally make a copy for themselves. Without this change, a person could have borrowed a program from a library or another individual, made an "archival" copy and retained it for his own use, thus engaging in the piracy that deprives the copyright owner of another sale.

The other effect of limiting the copying rights to the "owner" of a copy of a program was to assure that the broader copyright provisions did not detract from the contracts or licenses that accompany so much software. That is, the purchaser/lessee of a licensed or leased program with tighter restrictions than those contained in the copyright law should not be allowed to escape the contractual obligations simply because the copyright law might otherwise allow what the license prohibits. Technically, the license or lease agreement allows the lessor/copyright owner to retain ownership of the program, assigning the purchaser the role of lessee who essentially borrows that program. Again, not being the owner, the purchaser/lessee must abide by the restrictions placed by the lessor/copyright owner who alone has authority to make *or authorize* the making of copies of the computer program.

Libraries. The role of libraries in making software accessible to students will undoubtedly become an important dimension in the larger educational experience provided by schools. Many of the problems that are likely to develop are yet to be discovered, let alone encountered. One of the first and most basic questions, however, is: "What can we do in the event that a student borrower damages or destroys the copy of a computer program we loaned to him? May we simply make another archival copy from the back-up copy we already have in our archives?" The answer is "Yes but . . . ." In most instances, software producers include in the manual or license agreement a provision for returning any damaged copies to them to be either repaired or replaced for the owner. That, of course, is a time-consuming process, given the time required for a two-way journey through the mail, in addition to whatever time the company takes to respond to the order. A reasonable solution, then, is for the library (or any owner for that matter) to make a *temporary* archival copy from the original archival copy, to be used until the repaired or replaced copy is received. Once the damaged copy has been replaced, however, with a working copy, the temporary archival copy should be destroyed, if the library or other user is to remain within the restrictions of Section 117. If library personnel are willing to risk the "proliferation of users" interpretation, they might choose to retain the second archival copy *in their archives*, keeping it in reserve for use the next time a lost or damaged copy needs replacement. But that second archival copy, if retained, must not be made available to borrowers at the same time the regular lending copy is available; if proliferation of copies is debatable, proliferation of users is not.

Librarians are already familiar with Section 109 of the Copyright Act, the section entitled "Limitations on Exclusive Rights: Reproduction by Libraries and Archives." The essence of this provision is that libraries may copy a particular copyrighted work (even a substantial part or the entire work) at the request of an individual doing research, so long as neither the library nor the individual intend or receive any "commerical advantage" from the duplicated copy. Libraries also have special dispensation to make copies for purposes of replacing a "damaged, deteriorating, lost, or stolen" work, if the library or archives has, "after a reasonable effort, determined that an unused replacement cannot be obtained at a fair price." In the light of such provisions, it seems likely that a library could make the necessary replacement copies of computer programs at such time as originals could no longer be purchased. At this very early stage in the development of microcomputers and their software, such a situation will occur much less often than it may in the future. It is, however, difficult to predict whether software will be susceptible to the same "out of print" status that can afflict printed matter. At the same time, software now being produced is designed with a mass user clientele in mind, whereas certain scholarly books or journals are not, increasing the need to photocopy the limited number of copies available so that scholars can access them. Again, whether there will eventually be produced software with highly specialized content and a very small potential number of users remains to be seen. In any event, the Section 108 provisions allowing copying for purposes of archival replacement and for personal use by researchers provides at least some indication of the boundaries within which libraries can handle their software collections.

One additional provision of Section 108(e)(1) qualifies the right to make complete copies of works for scholarship and research by adding the requirement that the library must have "no notice that the copy . . . would be used for any purpose other than private study, scholarship, or research." This provision relieves libraries of liability for uses made of copies by users who requested and received those copies, unless the abuse is sufficiently blatant that the library had reason to suspect or know of its existence. How problematic this becomes in the future remains to be seen. On the one hand, it is easy to suspect any user of borrowing a copy of a computer program in order to make his own copy of it. On the other hand, the alternative seems to be to prohibit any owner from lending a copy of a program to anyone else.

All of the above assumes that the library *owns* its lending copies. Leased or licensed copies could be more problematic, unless the library negotiates a license to loan its purchased copies. A producer might well be willing to negotiate such an arrangement with an educational library. Absent the agreement, however, library personnel should be cautious, since some licenses limit the use of their programs to a specified machine.

Consequences of infringing. Sections 501 through 510 of the copyright law pertain to copyright infringement and remedies, with Sections 502-504 containing provisions for injunctions, for impounding and disposing of infringing articles, and for damages and profits. Of primary concern to educators is the provision pertaining to the damages for which an infringer can be liable. Specifically, if found guilty of copyright infringement, the guilty party is liable for "(1) the copyright owner's actual damages and any additional profits of the infringer, . . . or (2) statutory damages. . . . " While educators are unlikely to earn any profits from whatever infringement they may be guilty of, they should be prepared, however, to reimburse the copyright owner for whatever profits were lost by the infringing activity. That may not amount to much, as school budgets go. But a copyright owner involved in litigation on this scope is much more likely to elect "instead of actual damages and profits, an award of statutory damages for all infringements involved in the action, with respect to any one work, for which any one infringer is liable individually, or for which any two or more infringers are liable jointly and severally, in a sum of not less than $250 or more than $10,000 as the court considers just."

Under certain conditions, willfull infringement can render the infringer liable for up to $50,000 in statutory damages, while unknowing infringement may reduce the liability to $100 at the court's discretion. Better still, the court "shall remit statutory damages in any case where an infringer believed and had reasonable grounds for believing that his or her use of the copyrighted work was a fair use under Section 107, if the infringer was: (1) an employee or agent of a nonprofit educational institution, library, or archives acting within the scope of his or her employment. . . . "

SUMMARY

Because the copyright law amendments of 1980 dealing with computer programs leave unanswered a number of questions raised by educators about legal use of computer software in the schools, we must expand the context for analyzing the practices from which those questions arise. We must identify and understand the legal principles or tests derived from years of applying copyright law to other types of copyrighted works. And we must search for the most current legal opinions pertaining to the application of these principles to computer software.

Though legal opinion is divided on the issue of how many archival copies may be made and retained for back-up use, what concerns educators more is making accessible copies to the maximum number of students. If their students utilize a given program sequentially, there is probably no great danger of copyright infringement. If, however, their students access simultaneously a given program, there is considerable danger of infringement based on proliferation of users, on the market effect (deprivation of income to the copyright owner), and on the intended use of the software.

Educators must furthermore be alert to the existence of any license or lease agreements that prescribe the uses of the purchased or leased programs. Such licenses or leases are frequently more restrictive than the copyright law, but their provisions are binding unless they contradict the copyright law itself, which is unlikely.

Finally, educators need to keep in mind that any guidelines offered at this point may be based on authoritative legal opinions, but that the newness in the legal realm reflects the newness in the technological field. Much, therefore, remains to be clarified in the future by the courts.

CHAPTER 5

CONTROLLING PIRACY IN THE SCHOOLS

"Piracy" is the catchword applied to extensive and illegal copying of computer programs in violation of copyright law. It is by no means limited to the schools, though whether it is more or less extensive in education than in home and business markets has not been and is not likely to be documented accurately.

The discussion here is limited to piracy in the schools. Eliminating piracy completely—while no doubt the fantasy of every software producer—is not a goal considered realistic. Minimizing piracy, however, is not only a realistic goal of the producers, but is also a genuine concern of many educators. How to minimize or control piracy, in fact, has already been the source of much discussion among and between educators and producers. Analysis of proposed and actual solutions reveals at least four major categories of approaches. Two of these are primarily the responsibility of educators, and the remaining two belong in the software producers' domain.

The four most commonly identified means of controlling or minimizing piracy in schools include:

(1) monitoring
(2) consciousness raising
(3) reducing the financial incentive/motivation
(4) improving the technology of copy-protection.

Monitoring and consciousness raising are essentially the responsibility of educators, and they are responsibilities that seem already to be accepted by the educators currently engaged in discussions of the piracy problem. Any form of monitoring, of course, poses the problems of who can and should monitor the attempts to make and use illegal copies, especially given the ease and unobtrusiveness with which those prohibited activities can be accomplished.

Past discussions of monitoring in the educational environment have focused primarily on self-monitoring by local district administrators and staff. Raising the level of awareness about copyright restrictions on software usage is a respnsibility shared by both local and state level educators or agencies. Reducing the financial incentive and continuing to refine the technology of software protection are outside the domain of educators. The former strategy is primarily within the scope of software producers, distributors, and vendors. To accomplish the latter strategy of improving the technological means for protecting software, producers must work cooperatively with those having the technological expertise, especially developers of computer hardware.

All four of these strategies are costly, in terms of both hours and dollars. The investment of time and money by each sector, however, is an investment sure to bring a return far greater than the present cost of piracy, which now subtracts from the profits and the quality of computer software. Whether piracy can be satisfactorily contained remains to be seen. Our optimism or pessimism about the eventual resolution of the piracy problem in education probably corresponds to our basic optimism or pessimism about human nature. Yet, those who are optimistic about the potential resolution of this problem cite several convincing reasons for their optimism.

First, both educators and software producers recognize that failure to resolve the problem of piracy will be mutually detrimental, if not devastating. To the extent that piracy goes unchecked, those investing in its development and sale will lose their well-earned and deserved profits and perhaps the return of their initial investment as well. Without a sufficient profit margin, developers will have little motivation to produce quality educational software, and the educational system will suffer. Both educators and producers, then, have something to lose. In reverse, both sectors have much to gain by measures to contain software piracy in the schools. The quest for an effective solution is always spurred when the parties involved each have a measure of self-interest in the enterprise—which constitutes one good reason for optimism about the eventual success of the endeavor to contain the extensiveness of piracy.

Second, educators at the state and local levels have already (and voluntarily) begun to develop policies and procedures to try to control piracy. While many corporations and individuals may be copying defiantly and openly (and, unfortunately, some educators as well), educators as a group seem conscientiously and almost surprisingly concerned about abiding by the copyright law. The several plans discussed below testify to their commitment to fair play.

WHAT EDUCATORS CAN DO

State Level Activities

State education agencies can, and some—such as Montana—have already begun to do so, advise local school districts to negotiate with suppliers for a *reasonably priced* back-up copy to the original purchased copy of given software. Educators would prefer, of course, to be provided with a free back-up copy, but most would willingly accept a compromise measure that involved only a nominal fee for the back-up. While suppliers might prefer that the schools pay full price for a second copy, the compromise of a reduced price back-up should be preferable to no sale at all if the alternative is a pirated copy.

State education agencies can further advise local school districts to negotiate for modified copies of educational software to be downloaded into an in-school network system. Speaking to this recommendation, Dan Dolan of the Montana education agency has suggested that schools should, perhaps, be willing to pay more than the list price for an instructional program to be used in a network. But the negotiated price should also represent a substantial saving over the price of buying a copy for each unit in the network system.

By way of influencing if not muscling, state education agencies can also advise local school districts to negotiate with their software suppliers for rights to duplicate from the purchased copy only the number of copies needed to service the number of teachers or computers in a particular school. Monitoring the schools' compliance with this kind of arrangement might be problematic, but perhaps states could add this to any current regulations that they periodically check for compliance.

These first three suggestions constitute specific agreements that schools might undertake on their own, but that many schools might not consider or act upon without specific encouragement from the state. Whether a state choses to require or recommend that schools negotiate agreements, such action would raise the awareness of school administrators to the possibility of acquiring the needed quantity of software without either paying a fortune they can't afford or taking the risks of pirating. Our third suggestion also included mention of the responsibility of monitoring the schools' compliance with any negotiated agreement to reproduce only the number of copies required to use their hardware capacity to the fullest extent. In a broader vein, state education agencies might take or accept the responsibility for generally monitoring software piracy in the schools.

State level monitoring of software piracy in the schools is a solution as difficult as it is controversial. But there are at least two reasons why education agencies at the state or intermediate level are more appropriate agencies to conduct such monitoring than are the local districts or the software producers themselves. First, a state agency is more likely to be a disinterested party than local schools, which would necessarily be conducting a self-monitoring activity. Second, a state agency has the "machinery" and system with which to oversee the monitoring function while software producers have neither the staff, the experience, nor really the obligation to conduct such monitoring. State agencies may legitimately argue that their staffs are already overloaded with responsibilities and undersupported with resources to fulfill those responsibilities. But if society is serious about resolving the piracy problem, it could, through the state legislative enactments and appropriations, remedy the problem of insufficient resources that would otherwise hinder adequate monitoring.

Another factor affecting the feasibility of state level monitoring of software piracy in the schools is the level of curricular or administrative monitoring of schools presently being conducted in each state. Highly centralized, regulatory state agencies could more readily monitor schools for software piracy than could decentralized states, for the very reason that the machinery (staff and procedures) is already in place. While some educators may argue that the states already allocate too many resources to regulatory activities, and that all monitoring should be conducted at the local level, the state is, in fact, a more disinterested party to conduct such monitoring. While that is not the sole rationale for assigning to the states responsibility for monitoring, an objective public agency is most likely to satisfy software producers and any interest groups in society concerned about controlling piracy in the educational environment.

Regulation may constitute a familiar and essential function of state agencies, but in education the state or its regional service agencies can provide invaluable and less controversial assistance to local school districts. State agencies wanting to contribute to the containment of piracy in the schools might well consider a role less regulatory and more constructive from the perspective of the educators with whom they work. Specifically, these state or intermediate level agencies could assume the responsibility for "consciousness raising" concerning copyright law, first of district administrators and then of teachers. This consciousness raising can be achieved by conducting seminars or in-service workshops for school personnel dealing with copyright law as it pertains to computer software. In Montana, the state education agency not only offers seminars on this topic, but has also distributed to every school district a monograph (*Elements of Computer Education,* 1983) intended to acquaint educators with options available to them for obtaining necessary quantities of software legally—thus minimizing the temptation to copy illegally. Although a number of professional organizations may be providing similar services, states are in the best position to reach all school districts within their boundaries. They are better equipped to exert influence first and authority later, if necessary.

Local District Level Efforts

At the local level, some districts have already initiated the kind of negotiation that we have just suggested should be encouraged if not required by the states. The Sarasota (Florida) public school system, for example, adopted a policy requiring that each person who authorizes the purchase of a specific computer program must show evidence of having negotiated with the publisher or supplier for some kind of relief from copyright restrictions. This procedure utilizes a form (see Appendix E) for recording information about the attempted negotiation: who was contacted, what options were discussed, and so forth. In their negotiations for licensing and purchasing arrangements, Sarasota school personnel inform the seller of their district policy prohibiting illegal copying and of their serious efforts to monitor the use of purchased or leased software within their schools. In return, they have successfully negotiated a variety of licensing arrangements. According to Warren Spurlin, deputy superintendent of the Sarasota County School District, the district has found software producers and suppliers receptive to such arrangements as: permitting the district to make an agreed upon number of duplicate copies of the purchased copy of a program; substantial reductions in the price of multiple copies (up to 50 percent in some cases for purchase of multiple copies of curriculum series of programs); and special prices for programs to be used in a mainframe-network system. Both educators and software producers who have entered into these and comparable types of agreements feel that a signficant factor in the negotiations is the demonstrated willingness and effort of the school districts to prevent illegal copying and to monitor the use of software within the school setting. Documentation in the form of adopted policies and procedures will, of course, be more convincing to software sellers than mere statements of good intentions.

The development and implementation of policies and procedures for preventing piracy within the school environment, then, is an activity that local school districts can and should pursue immediately. Once educators recognize that such policies and procedures can result in direct financial savings and expanded software usage for their investment, they may cease to regard such activity as yet another bureaucratic obligation consuming administrative or educational time and energy better spent on other tasks.

School districts looking for assistance in the development of an effective policy for controlling piracy might begin with a document entitled "Suggested District Policy on Software Copyright." This model policy was included in the International Council for Computers in Education (ICCE) *Policy Statement on Network and Multiple Machine Software*, approved in June 1983 by the ICCE Board of Directors and later adopted by all members of the ICCE consortium. The significance of the adoption of this policy statement is that a large proportion of the educators in this country belong to organizations that recognize this policy. That alone will not put an end to piracy, but it is one indication among many that educators—teachers, administrators, and staff—will eventually become more aware of what needs to be done, what can be done, and where they can turn for assistance. A school district that adopted the ICCE policy would agree, among other things: to teach in every school the ethical and practical questions arising from software piracy; to forbid the use or making of illegal copies of copyrighted programs with school equipment; to refuse legal or insurance protection to employees who violate copyright laws; to assign responsibility for signing license agreements with software vendors to only one district level administrator, and to assign to the principal of each school building the responsibility for developing procedures to enforce the policy. The complete text of the policy statement, containing the suggested district policy, is found in the Appendix B. An additional practice recommended by Bobbie Goodsen, current president of Computer Using Educators (CUE) of California, is for school districts to make all back-up, archival copies in the district's central office.

The ICCE Suggested District Policy on Software Copyright not only provides educators with specific ideas for controlling piracy in their schools, but as mentioned above, its district-individualized version could also be used by school districts in their attempts to negotiate with software distributors beneficial terms for purchase or licensing agreements. Software suppliers have demonstrated their willingness to negotiate reasonable purchase and license agreements for single or multiple copies when presented with evidence of schools' commitment to controlling piracy. This willingness has been indicated in specific negotiated agreements with school districts around the country. It was particularly evident in the 1983 Conference on Producer-Educator Perspectives on Educational Software, sponsored by the National Institute of Education and the Association for Educational Communications and Technology.

Teacher In-Service on Copyright Law

One of the prerequisites to complying with a law is, of course, knowledge and understanding of that law. Copyright law is not a law with which many teachers have had reason to be familiar—until the last decade. With "a Xerox machine in every school," the legal limitations of photocopying have become familiar indirectly through the guidelines for classroom copying that were developed to clarify the fair use Section 107 of the 1976 Copyright Act. Any teachers or school districts previously inclined to take lightly the copyright restrictions must have been "converted" to the advisability of adhering to those restrictions, however, by the action taken against New York University and the eight professors who had blatantly disregarded the copyright law and guidelines for printed materials. Those guidelines, however, have little direct relevance for computer software.

There are numerous ways of informing teachers and other educators about the software copyright law. But the mode that is most likely to have an impact is an in-service program where the material can be conveyed with the full force of a personal presentation. Merely placing a photocopy of Section 117 in the mailbox of each teacher will never suffice; and a copy of the complete text of the copyright law would have even less impact because of the quantity and specialization of the material. Written copies of the pertinent sections may be useful as a reference, once teachers are familiar with the essential elements of the law. But that familiarity depends heavily on all the creativity, guile, and ability to convince that an effective speaker can bring to a discussion of the legalities of software piracy.

Whose responsibility is it to initiate and provide these in-service programs? While the school board/school committee should be concerned about the problem, it is primarily the responsibility of the central administration to initiate a teacher in-service on software copyright. That follows naturally from their responsibility in developing or adopting a policy to control illegal software copying. The central office may delegate to the building principals the responsibility for providing in-service on copyright for their teachers and staff, but the financing of a quality program probably requires a district-wide program for all but the largest, urban school districts.

Where can administrators turn for assistance in locating or presenting in-service programs on software copyright? To some extent, that will depend upon the level and sophistication of state leadership in this field. Some state or intermediate level education agencies may already have developed programs or materials for raising the level of awareness of educators in their state or region. In other states, educational computer consortia may fill that function. Occasionally, institutions of higher learning may provide excellent resources, for many of the copyright experts are affiliated with universities. There are also a number of professional organizations becoming involved in the effort to educate educators about the appropriate and legal uses of computer software in the schools. AECT, the Association for Educational Communications and Technology, produces both written and audiovisual materials to provide vital information about copyright law as it affects the use of software in the educational setting.

WHAT SOFTWARE PRODUCERS AND PUBLISHERS CAN DO

There are two major strategies for reducing or controlling software piracy that are most reliant on the software suppliers for initiation and/or implementation. One, the technological approach, requires a cooperative venture with the hardware producers to develop an encryption process or other protective strategy that protects the software without rendering it too inflexible. The technological strategy is costly, it is frustrating to those who try to design the technological protection devices, and its fruits are far from foolproof. As soon as a new program with a new copy-protection scheme is released, users with lots of time and motivation (hobbyists and high school and college students) begin their game of "cracking" or "breaking" the code or system. According to Brian Lee of Synapse Software, the best efforts of his company to stymie unauthorized copying seldom protect a program for more than three or four weeks (*Wall Street Journal,* 9/6/83). Yet, computer technologists will continue to search for the most effective technological processes to prevent copying of the programs that will deprive copyright owners, often the parent computer company, of profits from the sale of their software.

One antipiracy measure includes the design of a computer program that searches for the serial number in the memory of the first computer on which it is operated; once that serial number has been identified, the program runs only the machine with that number. The liability of this tactic, of course, is that the owner of such a program loses the program if his or her computer dies or is sold or traded for a newer model at some point in the future.

Other technological strategies involve the encasement of software in protective modules. Atari and Texas Instruments have tried this approach, enclosing their software on a read-only memory chip rather than on tape or disk. The problem with this approach is the expense involved in manufacturing the encased software; in order to recover the high cost, producers must aim for large volume sales, which tends to result in the lowest common denominator in terms of instructional quality of the software. Manufacturers of software using the mouse, a hand-held controller, in place of a keyboard are experimenting with a design that allows a specific program copy to be operated by only the one mouse electronically embedded with the same serial number as the program sold with it. As sophisticated and impressive as that sounds, Daniel Fylstra of VisiCorp, which markets such a program, describes it as no panacea but "just another tactic."

The other type of strategy heavily dependent upon software producers for successful reduction of piracy is the development of a variety of negotiated arrangements with educators for the purchase or lease of software. Since software suppliers have a vested interest in reducing the amount of piracy that robs them of profits, they, like educators, have shown a willingness to negotiate. It may be unrealistic to expect them to initiate some of the arrangements described below, at least during this early phase of educational microcomputing. The temptation must be strong to "let the buyer beware." That is, if a school district is sophisticated enough to intiate purchase or leasing negotiations, many suppliers will engage in those negotiations. But if a school district is inexperienced or uninformed about the potential for negotiations, most suppliers are unlikely to volunteer a discount rate for multiple or back-up copies, for example. This situation is but another dimension of the transitional nature of software problems that currently affect the schools. If only a portion of the school personnel purchasing software are currently aware of their potential negotiating powers, it is only a matter of time until most educators will share this awareness.

One of the most problematic aspects of the acquisition of instructional software is the need for back-up or archival copies. So vital and legitimate is this need, in fact, that it is one of the two legally sanctioned justifications specified in computer software copyright law for making a copy of a computer program. The fragility of floppy disks renders them vulnerable to a variety of abuses, accidental or intentional. When a school district has paid $30 to $300 or more for a computer program, there must be some kind of "insurance" against destruction of that program due to dropped keys, wayward magnets, spilled coffee, or other simple fumbling. It is that "insurance" function that is served by a back-up copy; if the master disk is destroyed, the back-up is available to become the new master disk.

A common complaint of school personnel—and a reason often given for making additional copies—is that suppliers do not provide back-up copies, at least not without an additional charge. This complaint is validated by the findings of the survey cited earlier (Hoover and Gould, 1982). Of the Apple software producers surveyed, 72 percent indicated that they provide no back-up copies with the initial purchase; only 3 percent provide one back-up with the purchase; another 3 percent provide a back-up upon request with no charge; and 22 percent provide back-up copies with an additional charge. Those who offer back-up copies for purchase generally charge only ten dollars, though the price ranges from $5 to $20. It seems reasonable to believe public school speakers who say that most school districts would willingly pay a nominal fee for back-up copies if that option were available to them. And making it available, as does Addison-Wesley, (Letellier, p. 44) is one way software producers could reduce the need or incentive to pirate copies of the purchased master disks.

A multiple copy discount constitutes another, closely related measure software producers could take to reduce the piracy of their programs in the schools. A school district with, for example, 150 microcomputers in classrooms can seldom afford to buy at retail cost the number of programs for each topic or skill to be used at each grade level with each computer. That district could, however, provide the necessary amount of software for its students if quantity purchasing resulted in reduced rates. Interestingly, of the Apple suppliers surveyed by Hoover and Gould, 82.5 percent indicated a willingness to negotiate a special price with a district for multiple copy purchases. As mentioned earlier, such willingness can only benefit those school districts knowledgeable about the option of negotiating in the first place. Once the option of negotiating becomes commonplace information, pressure will be on suppliers to advertise their multiple-copy pricing schemes. One more of the transitional aspects of the piracy problem will have been alleviated, if not eliminated.

A different approach to negotiation has been successfully tried by a number of school districts that had the advantage of early involvement in computer-assisted instruction. Some of their staff had acquired sufficient programing sophistication to develop quality software for use in their own schools. Later, district personnel were able to negotiate an exchange of their locally developed software in return for an agreed amount of commercially developed software. This option, of course, while theoretically available to all school districts, is limited in its potential to those districts or educational units with staff who can create or who have created some exceptionally high quality software. As the general quality and quantity of software better fits the needs of schools, this may become even less an option than it is now, but during this transitional period it can provide interesting and profitable opportunities for some school districts.

Although much software negotiation now occurs between suppliers and individual school districts, some state level agencies have negotiated agreements, especially with such hardware/software manufacturers as IBM, Apple, Radio Shack, and others, to make software available to school districts at discount rates ranging from 10 percent to 30 percent. Still another possibility is the negotiation of discounted quantity purchases by educational computer consortia. Whatever the agency, software suppliers willing to negotiate discounts for quantity purchasing will contribute to the solution of their profit-robbing piracy problem.

Still another approach to minimizing piracy is to negotiate licensing agreements. Science Research Associates (SRA) promotes licensing agreements that involve a contract in which the client agrees not to copy purchased disk software. Both the contract and the disk are imprinted with the same licensing number, enabling SRA to trace illicit copies back to the original purchaser. Although some people are skeptical of the effectivness of this approach, SRA believes that their licensing policy is successful, if only as a psychological deterrent. It also serves to raise the level of awareness about copyright law.

A variation on the licensing approach to controlling software piracy is the type of licensing agreement proposed by CUE, the California-based Computer Using Educators. The policy they recommend calls for the leasing of programs to a school, which would be allowed to reproduce the number of copies needed to service all teachers in that school. While this may strike software producers as unrealistically lenient, there are other variations on this theme that might be more acceptable.

MECC (Minnesota Educational Computing Consortium) leases its entire software collection to institutional members. Those members, with increasing frequency, are state education agencies or intermediate education agencies within states, though individual school districts are eligible for membership. As institutional members, agencies or school districts pay a pre-established fee for the cost of leasing copy-protected software. Along with the copy-protected software, institutional members receive a copy program with which they can make additional copy-protected copies for schools located in their jurisdiction. MECC has reason to believe that this approach will minimize the amount of piracy committed with their software. Furthermore, institutional members may determine their own pricing policies. But whether they make the software available free of charge or at a nominal fee, the schools they service have access to quality software at a fraction of the cost of commercially marketed programs. The very reasonableness or affordability of the prices paid further reduces the perceived or real "need" to pirate copies in order to provide sufficient software. Producers may choose not to price their products competitively with the products of nonprofit software producers. The MECC approach to licensing, nevertheless, merits their serious consideration. At least one educational software company has, in fact, announced its own variation of a MECC-type licensing arrangement (Zientara, p. 5). Bertamax, located in Seattle, Washington, encourages schools to form a consortium with a minimum of 50 schools, one of which is designated as the "consortium host." The host is provided with a complete set of 250 program disks (not 250 programs) and accompanying teachers' manuals. Bertamax licenses the host to duplicate unlimited numbers of copies of the courseware for its member schools, which are to be charged $500 the first year and $250 annually thereafter. For that $500 fee, the school is essentially paying only $2.00 per disk. Compared to the prices charged by many commerical publishers for a series of lessons, this represents a savings of hundreds of dollars *per series*. Needless to say, with access to such vast quantities of software for such nominal fees, there is simply no need to make illegal duplicate copies in order to save money.

Finally, software producers could adopt another strategy to limiting piracy of their products. Following the example of MicroPro, producer of *Wordstar*, software developers can simply market "open" copies of their software, i.e., programs without any copy-protection device at all. Any incentive for buying rather than pirating such software stems from the emphasis on user support, in the form of frequent software updates made available only to registered owners of the product. Edward Currie, President of Lifeboat Associates software publishing company in New York, believes this to be a more enlightened approach to containing illegal copying. Optimistically, he predicts that serious users of such software will reject continued use of pirated copies when they see the advantages of owning legitimate copies. MicroPro, however, has refrained from technological copy-protection more because they have not yet found an adequate effective system than because of a decision *not* to copy-protect their products.

Software producers and suppliers, we have seen, may choose from a wide variety of strategies for protecting their investment in the development and marketing of educational software. No one approach will eliminate illegal copying; not even the adoption of numerous strategies simultaneously will put an end to piracy. But each strategy has been found effective by some companies in their efforts to protect their programs and their profits. Certainly there will be creative and determined developers who will continue to experiment with technological devices for preventing illegal copying. And just as certainly, commerical suppliers will find themselves adjusting their prices to reflect educators' needs for multiple and back-up copies.

WHAT EDUCATORS, SOFTWARE PRODUCERS AND PUBLISHERS CANNOT DO

Many aspects of the piracy problem are, as we have established, transitional in nature. Our response cannot be, however, to wait out the transition. Some analysts have recommended that we wait for the free market solution to piracy. That is, let the low quality software be forced out of the market by the high quality software and let the overpriced software either be forced out of the market by the moderately priced competition or else survive by the necessary price reduction. This free market competition will undoubtedly occur and make its impact. But it is a relatively slow and unreliable solution. The schools need quality software affordably priced now . . . not a decade from now. And there are too many examples of social and business problems that will never be resolved by free enterprise alone to warrant the heavy reliance on this nonsolution.

The legal system, too, will play a role in the solution to the piracy problem. But it is even slower and more limited in scope and effectiveness than the free market system. Hardware and software producers at this time are limiting their legal tactics to the wholesale pirates and to the internal systems software pirating that was the focus, for example, of *Apple v. Franklin*. To bring suit against an individual making an illegal copy in his or her home or school is more costly than effective. That is not to say that at some time, a software supplier may not follow in the path of the publishers who sued New York University and a private copy center for violating the fair use section of the copyright law protecting the printed medium. But this strategy will never comprise a major part of the effort to contain illegal copying of computer programs.

Finally, the transitional nature of the piracy problem does not allow educators or software producers to wait for the technological solution. As sophisticated as is the technology of computer hardware and as sophisticated as software is becoming, none of the industry speakers today believe that technology will ever provide a crack-proof code or a fool-proof device to prevent copying. Again, advances will be made and experimentation will continue, but no one is confident that the technological solution will become the ultimate solution—and most certainly not during this transitional period.

In short, the technological, legal, and free market solutions may play minor roles in society's effort to control software piracy but each of these approaches is slow, costly, and at best only partially effective. Educators cannot afford to wait for these solutions to make possible reasonably priced, quality educational software. Nor can software producers wait for these solutions to protect their investments and profits during the transition.

WHAT SOCIETY CAN DO

The burden of reducing the extensiveness of piracy, especially in the schools, rests heavily, as we have seen, with educators and software producers themselves. Though they are the sectors with the most to gain from a resolution of the piracy problem, society, too, stands to benefit. To some extent, any progress made in containing piracy in the school setting cannot help but affect the containment of software piracy in other sectors of society. Likewise, solutions for controlling piracy in the home or business markets cannot but help to further the cause of containing piracy in the educational environment. For that reason, those who shape national policy have some responsibility to contribute to the resolution of this complex problem.

Whether or not the federal government should become more deeply involved in anything affecting American education is a forever hotly debated topic. One relatively uncontroversial role it could play, however, would be to bring together parties interested in the development of guidelines for software use in the schools, comparable, perhaps, to the Guidelines for Off-Air Recording of Broadcast Programming for Educational Purposes and the Guidelines for Classroom Copying in Not-for-Profit Educational Institutions. It is with some reluctance that anyone supportive of the educators' perspective should recommend this action, for both sets of guidelines are perceived by many educators to be almost suffocatingly restrictive and detrimental to the educational enterprise. Best to let sleeping dogs lie, they are inclined to feel. The trouble with sleeping dogs is that they wake up, and they may be cranky upon waking!

Without more specific guidelines for using software in the schools, educators will continue to feel insecure about their practices in utilizing computer software. If the suggested guidelines were developed by representatives from the various interest groups such as educators, software developers, software producers, publishing houses, and hardware manufacturers, educators would gain considerable insight into the problem and perspectives of others. They might better understand several of the legal principles that now go so far toward protecting the copyright owners. With this understanding, they might avoid some of the most problematic or obviously offensive uses. With such guidelines, they might also avoid lengthy and costly confrontations in court.

Whether the Department of Education, Congress, the Copyright Office, or some other agency should take the initiative in bringing together the representatives of the appropriate interest groups to develop guidelines for software use in the schools must be determined first. A disinterested, authoritative body to whom the deliberating body would be accountable seems to suggest Congress as the "prime mover." Once it authorized the establishment of a commission, however, it could delegate responsibility to the National Institute of Education, for example, for constituting and overseeing the deliberations of that commission similar to the relationship between the NIE and the National Commission on Excellence in Education.

At the state level, society could effect greater containment of piracy in the schools through legislative enactments and appropriations for monitoring activities conducted by state education agencies. This additional bureaucratic, regulatory function will not be welcomed by educators, however, and a better variation might call for primary reliance on self-monitoring by local school personnel with only occasional audits by state agencies.

Finally, society may need to come to terms with its responsibility in helping to resolve the problem of piracy in sectors other than education. Of course, "society" soon translates into "government" and governmental prevention or control of piracy easily translates into additional governmental regulation, an unhappy response from the perspective of everyone—including the software producers themselves.

CHAPTER 6

INSTRUCTIONAL SOFTWARE IN THE SCHOOLS: KEEPING THE SCHOOL MARKET ALIVE

The health of the school market for instructional software in this transitional phase of the 1980s cannot be diagnosed as robust, though assessments vary concerning its present and future condition. If educators and software producers alike are concerned about the vitality of the school market, few are keeping a death watch. Since both sectors have a vested interest in bolstering that market against the onslaught of "childhood diseases" and accidents that can retard its growth or even threaten its life, they need to begin attending to the technological equivalent of an immunization program. At the present time, threre are three potentially crippling diseases that could weaken or even kill the school market, depending upon several variables. Those three threats to the health of the school market are (1) the quality factor, (2) the piracy factor, and (3) the home market factor. Each of these factors will be discussed in terms of the potential severity of the threat it poses and in relation to preventive measures that may "immunize" the school market to that threat.

THE QUALITY FACTOR

The currently dismal quality of most instructional software has led some to predict that educational personnel will become sufficiently discouraged about its classroom effectiveness to abandon CAI altogether. The now rapidly multiplying microcomputers, they forecast, will be relegated eventually to the same storage closets as technological predecessors touted in their time for their potential to revolutionize education. A few disillusioning encounters with user-unfriendly or instructionally unsatisfying software can provide teachers with more than enough justification to reject computers they were skeptical about in the first place. Even open-minded educators willing to share their instructional roles with computers may lose the motivation and commitment to work at integrating the computer into the classroom environment. Poor quality software can also "turn off" students now so entranced with the novelty of the computer. Frustration and boredom lurk just behind functionally deficient or repetitive programs. And once students lose interest—admittedly a response more likely to be delayed than teacher disillusionment—it may be extraordinarily difficult to regain or recapture their enthusiasm.

What can be done to prevent this potential threat from materializing? First of all, educators must understand that the poor quality of much educational software today is not a generic defect of that software. Rather, poor quality is a natural if regrettable limitation of a newly developing product—a problem that is largely transitional in nature. More specifically, educators must realize that many of the pedagogical and functional deficiencies of today's software are a result of programs written by noneducator programers eager to capitalize on a young market. This limitation will be corrected when both the developers and the users of educational software become more experienced and sophisticated. With experience, educator-users will become informed and critical consumers, rather than hungry buyers grabbing for the first and sometimes the only special function program available on the market.

The ability of teachers to function as educated consumers will improve as they utilize or try out a variety of programs and as they read rapidly developing evaluative literature available from such nonprofit agencies as Consumers Union [*Consumer Reports,* 1983], EPIE/Consumers Union in New York, (see *Consumer Reports,* November 1983), Conduit in Iowa City, and the Educational Software Evaluation Consortium in California, composed of representatives of 17 of the most respected software evaluation agencies in the nation. As the knowledge and experience of users will ensure greater demand for quality software, so the knowledge and experience of producers should eventually minimize many of the programing "bugs" that now detract from much educational software.

With the passage of time, more educators can be expected to develop expertise and interest in creating educational software, though they have to leave the field of teaching if they are to become involved in serious software development. Few teachers have sufficient time or energy to invest in the rigors of creating quality software. While the majority of educators will probably never develop that level of interest, others will at least be able to function as consultants and field evaluators with noneducator developers. Even "average" or typical classroom teachers should eventually be able to provide intelligent and informed feedback to producers about what they want, what they like, what works, what doesn't work, and why. Obviously these developments will take time. If educators realize this, and recognize that many of the current deficiencies in educational software need not be more than transitory, they will have taken a significant step away from permanent disillusionment.

Secondly, local school boards, committees, and school administrators have a responsibility to provide teachers with training in the use of computer hardware and software. Teachers collectively are overworked, underpaid, and frequently disinclined to become familiar with computers and how the computer can be incorporated into their classrooms. In order to provide the multidimensional support system for teachers to become skilled computer users, administrators must themselves develop knowledge about computers and skills in CAI. Numerous studies have documented that the quality of administrative leadership is a determining factor in the success or failure of any major project involving curricular change or development.

The integration of the computer into the learning environment of the schools constitutes one of the greatest challenges to those responsible for curriculum and instruction. For that reason, it is imperative that administrators initiate in-service training for teachers and staff, or at the very least respond to state level initiation of such training. It is equally imperative that such in-service efforts not end where they often begin—with a one-session afternoon seminar. "It must be an ongoing program that raises the level of competency of all the staff and keeps them somewhat abreast of this fast-moving, changing technology: [*The Elements of Computer Education,* p. 101].

Once administrators have acquired some degree of computer literacy, they will be in a better position to facilitate for their staffs an awareness of the hardware and software available, an understanding of the uses to which the computer can be put, and the ability to evaluate software for its effectiveness in achieving selected goals in the classroom. Only as teachers become familiar with a variety of programs will they acquire the perspective to know what works and for what purposes. This knowledge will help them select the best of what is available, as well as provide the kind of feedback to software producers that will enable them to develop the most appropriate and effective software for the classroom.

Greater familiarity with the types of instructional software available will further enable teachers to structure the total learning environment to maximize the potential of the best software. Again, everyone should bear in mind that the acquisition of this familiarity with and knowledge about computer hardware and software will not occur simultaneously with the arrival of the computer—it will take a number of years. Accepting this time limitation can provide both educators and software producers with the patience and perspective necessary while living with the frustrations of this transitional phase.

And how are educators to acquire the knowledge and skills to evaluate, select, use, and provide feedback on instructional software? Their need to learn and apply evaluative criteria and to learn how to restructure the classroom learning environment for the integration of computer-assisted instruction requires the guidance of experienced and knowledgeable users of educational software. One of the most viable and most effective modes of introducing teachers and other educators to computer hardware and software is through training courses and workshops. Such training is becoming increasingly available through educational computer consortia, continuing education courses at the university level, state educational agencies, publishers and hardware/software manufacturers, and professional associations such as AECT. These various organizations collectively will bring about the computer literacy for teachers that so many young people have "naturally" acquired because these youngsters have not only the innate curiosity, but also the time to indulge in satisfying it. Computer literacy for teachers, of course, means something more complex and sophisticated than is meant by computer literacy for students or for the general public. Because it entails so much more than simply using a program in a machine, computer literacy for teachers, like professional development, will never be a destination so much as a journey. And as professional development is furthered by continuing education, in-service training, and workshops, so the effective use of computers in the classroom will be similarly advanced.

Educators have a responsibility to respond to the frequently reiterated complaint of educational software producers that teachers either don't know what they want, or at the least do not convey to the producers what they want for use in the classoom. The fact is that many teachers may not be sure of what they want at this point, having had little if any experience with computer-assisted or computer-managed instruction. However, as they acquire familiarity with both hardware and software as we expect, they should discover what they want. At that point, they should convey to software suppliers their preferences. Purchasing trends will also indicate to producers what teachers want and what they consider effective in the classroom. Software developers should keep in mind that as teachers gain expertise with one type of software, *e.g.*, drill-and-practice routines, they may want for themselves and their students more stimulating types of software, such as simulations and problem solving programs. But here again we are describing a relatively slow, evolutionary process—not an instant solution to a troublesome problem.

Just as educators have a number of responsibilities in solving the software quality problem to help keep the school market alive, so too do software developers have similar responsibilities. It is more difficult to generalize about those responsibilities because of the diversity in types of software suppliers. Some are nonprofit firms, some are textbook publishers, some are personal computer manufacturers, some are game firms, and so on. When referring to profit-making corporations, it is also difficult to speak of their "responsibilities" when their primary function or responsibility is understood to be the turning of a profit. Nevertheless, many of the following suggestions are applicable to commercial, proprietary developers and especially to textbook publishers expanding their domains into the realm of computer software.

Rather than speak of responsibilities of software producers, it may be more appropriate to suggest those actions that will lead to long term profits and the preservation of the school market. Preserving the market constitutes a responsibility of sorts, and may be the most difficult suggestion to act upon. Long range vision, in the American experience, tends to describe the foresight that extends into the next business quarter; and this short-sightedness inevitably results in products that have more "come on" power than staying power. Yet studies of the most *successful* American businesses and industries, to say nothing of their Japanese counterparts, reveal that a consistent and essential trait in achieving success is the ability for management to develop long range goals and strategies. So in a sense, our suggestion that software developers have a responsibility to balance their short term profit goals with long term vision is merely asking them to follow a strategy that is in their own best interest.

One of the long term strategies commercial developers of educational software should adopt in their effort to resolve the quality problem affecting the health of the school market is to involve more educators in the development of their software. Here they might consider the practice of MECC, whose software is developed by teams of programers and designers who are expected to have four to six years of classroom teaching experience. Whether commercial producers choose to add educators to their teams of staff or whether they choose to involve educators in a consulting capacity, they must remedy the current lack of programer awareness about the way children learn. Involving educators at the earliest stages of program development, an apparently costly measure, would actually save time and money in the long run. Waiting until the field test or pilot phase to learn of instructional deficiencies or flaws is extremely costly. Criticism is also less acceptable after great quantities of time and money have been invested. Pilot testing or field testing should be a vital part of software development, but the likelihood of major changes being required at that stage is substantially reduced if well-prepared educators have seen and reacted to earlier versions.

Software developers seeking additional ways to remedy flaws in educational software might consider training for themselves. Workshops or seminars on child development or principles of learning theory might be enlightening, as would short-term, intensive dialogues with educators having experience and sophistication in software development. But it is unlikely that this approach can even be as effective as one based on early and continual dialogue with educators in whatever capacity producers might finally select.

Another responsibility of software developers is to provide or upgrade supplementary and complementary instructional materials—what MECC and others term "courseware." Courseware generally includes instructions for and uses of software. In addition to improving the quality of this documentation, producers must begin to develop the kinds of supplementary materials and manuals that textbook producers develop and provide to accompany books. Lists of related readings and resources, instructional objectives, exercises, suggested activities, assignments, and tests will make the software itself much more attractive to teachers who are accustomed to receiving such supplementary material with textbooks. Again, implementation of this suggestion would be costly, but perhaps more cost-effective in the long run. Educators object less to high prices of software than to the prices *for what they get*. Quality programs accompanied by quality instructional materials should bring far fewer complaints about overpricing than now occur. And of course when a school district is buying software, multiple copies of programs need not necessarily entail multiple copies of related courseware materials.

THE PIRACY FACTOR

Illegal copying of computer software in the schools is a practice that repeatedly is cited by commercial software producers and publishers as a potential reason for abandoning the school market. If they cannot obtain a fair return on their investments, they argue, they will simply have to stop producing instructional software for the schools. But despite these predictions or warnings, there is reason to doubt the likelihood of such a development. Why? Because, first of all, piracy is in no way limited to the school environment. If anything, some analysts and even some software producers suspect much higher rates of piracy in the business and home markets. Certainly there is no consensus or general feeling that piracy is any greater in the schools than in homes or businesses. Yet one never hears threats that the future of software for business or for personal management or entertainment purposes is threatened because of piracy, however rampant. True, the current and potential school market may be smaller than either of the other two marketing sectors. But it is not an insignificant market for developers who are committed to producing quality educational software. The universality of the piracy problem, then, suggests that the health and future of the school market is at best only slightly more threatened by piracy than the home and business markets.

Another reason to react cautiously to predictions of the death of instructional software for the schools is the history of copyright problems with everything from player piano rolls to phonograph records, audiocassette tapes, and videocassette recorders. Misuse and abuse of copyright limitations on recording of television programs—especially motion pictures—has not prevented motion picture and television producers from producing their movie and TV shows. Likewise, audiotaping of records and of other cassette tapes, while it may have eaten into the profits of recording artists and vendors, has not jeopardized the existence of the recording industry itself. And those entertainment industries to not have the option available to software producers of building in the same kind of technological copy-protecting devices—however limited their effectiveness.

Software producers might consider the kinds of alternatives being considered to protect television and motion picture producers from excessive profit losses due to video recorders. Specifically, a levy could be added to the price of the software (and perhaps even to the hardware), the proceeds of which would be directed to the producers to offset some of the losses accruing from the illegal reproduction of their products. This alone, of course, will neither prevent piracy nor entirely reimburse producers for their lost profits. It also has the liability of requiring some agency to determine which producers should receive how much of the revenues raised by such a levy. And, of course, buyers will balk at yet another user tax. That may be one price society should expect to pay, however, for the privilege of cheap and easy access to the desirable products of others' creativity.

Other measures that can be taken to prevent piracy from jeopardizing the future of the school software market include those discussed in the previous chapter on piracy control. A quick review would highlight the efforts of educators to raise the level of awareness about copyright law and its implications for educational software; school district efforts to develop and enforce self-monitoring procedures; and mutual efforts by educators and software producers to negotiate reduced prices for backup copies, for multiple copy purchases, and for exchanges made involving locally produced software. Commercial producers might even consider their own variations on MECC's leasing arrangement, whereby its entire software collection is leased to institutional members. These may be state educational agencies, intermediate/regional agencies within the states, or even school districts for schools not located in either an intermediate state agency region or a state with institutional membership. Again in this model, copy-protected software is accompanied by a copy program with which the member can make additional copies that are themselves also copy-protected. These copies may be made by the state or intermediate educational agency at the request of member school districts, or by the school district having institutional membership at the request of school personnel within the district. But commercial software suppliers need not restrict their vision to the nonprofit sector, for they now can look to Bertamax in Seattle as a model for providing large quantities of software at nominal prices under the conditions of a licensing arrangement. Options are numerous and provide many different approaches to overcoming the piracy factor.

THE HOME MARKET FACTOR

As personal computers become a part of daily life in ever more homes, some producers of educational software suggest that piracy problems in the school market may force them to develop their instructional software for the home user rather than for the classroom user. After all, they correctly maintain, there are many more homes than there are schools or even classrooms. Quality Education Data, Inc. (QED) projects that while the education market will continue to grow in terms of the number of microcomputers being used in the schools, "because of the limited market size and saturation [it] will comprise less than 5 percent of total number of units" [*Micrompuier Data,* p. 1]. Of the four markets identified by QED, only the scientific market is smaller than education; both the home and business markets are and will remain dramatically larger than education. The number of machines in use is only one factor in sizing up the future market for instructional software, but it gives some indication of the potential. And software producers are not threatening to abandon the instructional software market entirely; they are simply suggesting that if profits cannot be made in developing and supplying educational software to the schools, there will certainly be profits for the development and marketing of educational software for the children of all those parents who either want to help their offspring get ahead or hope to help their children catch up.

This possibility may sound convincing at first. And at least one experienced educator, Leroy Finkel, has recently observed that:

> Already . . . I have seen a subtle change take place in the educational software market. Two years ago, publishers and developers designed software for schools and then produced a derivative product for the home-education market. These products tended to have sound teaching pedagogy and reflected the same subjects we taught in school. Now, since profits seem to be higher in the home-education market, publishers are designing software for the home market with derivative products being produced for the school. These new products are much more "gamey" and entertaining and relate less and less to the subjects we teach [Finkel, 1983].

But then a number of questions surface, and many of those questions stem from the nature of much instructional software. Most programs focus on the development of just one relatively simple skill or one relatively narrow concept or body of information. Once mastered, there is no reason to continue using that program. In other words, much instructional software is susceptible to quick obsolescence for the original, individual user. This short life span of any given instructional program has serious ramifications for home users. First of all, parents will catch on quickly to the potential cost of educating or tutoring their children via computer if programs are not priced very cheaply. If educational software is designed well enough to attract and retain family users at all, the latter are likely to turn to a variety of lending and exchange organizations for acquisition of software. There are already user group exchanges where individuals or families pay a nominal fee for membership, and then either lease, borrow, or swap programs at will. Should the existence of such groups be legally challenged, there will still be the option of a variety of software libraries—public libraries with software collections added to their other media collections, public school libraries, and perhaps proprietary lending agencies as well. Whether or not they will cut into the home market depends on the pricing patterns that develop. Certainly the lending of stereo records from public libraries has hardly put the record industry out of business . . . but then, records don't cost what computer programs cost at the present.

It has been suggested that educational software is analogous to encyclopedias, and the inference follows that educational software like encyclopedias can service both the home and the school markets. The analogy is intriguing, and seems to be based on the similar function of both encyclopedia and instructional software as a source of information made available to students both in school libraries and in the homes of parents who value their children's educational development. Furthermore, we are likely to find the wide range in the quality of encyclopedias on the market to be paralleled by an equally wide range in the quality of instructional software. In the case of encyclopedias, this variation is only partly the result of attempts to design various encyclopedias for a variety of age levels and uses. From the original immense, dense, scholarly, and expensive Encyclopaedia Britannica, the expanded marketplace is now filled with supermarket varieties of alphabetized picture books containing one paragraph discussions written to entertain an eight year old. Yet the presence of encyclopedias in the home, of whatever quality or variety, has not for a moment jeopardized the school market. Children use the encyclopedia for specific assignments and sometimes out of general curiosity—in either setting. But the encyclopedia is used as one of many tools available for enriching the learning experience provided by both home and school.

Here is where the notion of the computer as a high tech encyclopedia raises some questions. Most analysts and even computer enthusiasts foresee the computer's role in education as primarily that of a tool, enriching and supplementing the instructional program designed and supervised by teachers. But the interactive capacity of the computer makes it eminently more captivating and engrossing than the encyclopedia, and that interactive capacity in turn assures a wider function than that of containing and dispensing information. The potential of computers for providing educational simulations, individualized skill building, problem solving activities, and so forth constitutes a major limitation in the computer-encyclopedia analogy.

Of all the projections about the effect of the home market on educational software, perhaps the most drastic is that the computer will render the schools all but obsolete, since learning will occur in the home via computer rather than in the school. While this is entirely feasible from a technological standpoint, it is just as entirely unfeasible from a social standpoint, for it fails to take into account the "babysitting factor." That is, the schools provide a supervised place for young people to spend their days while parents work, in or out of the home. How many parents would ever embrace an educational program based in their homes? If employed, they would have to hire someone to supervise their children or abandon their concerns about the safety of their children and property alike. Parents not employed outside the home would hardly cheer an arrangement that kept their preadolescent or adolescent children under their skins and feet on a daily basis. The children, furthermore, would sorely miss the socializing that makes even the oft-complained-about compulsory education appealing by the end of a long, unstructured, or possibly isolated summer. Society, in short, would be decidedly disrupted by a population of young people left to their own devices, day after day, without the educational and social structure provided by the schools. Those who fantasize about computerized home instruction have simply failed to come to terms with the logistics of such a scenario.

The home market for educational software is undoubtedly a market to be reckoned with, from the standpoint of the schools, and a market to be courted from the standpoint of the software producers. But the very nature of individualized, unassisted computer instruction is radically different from the computerized instruction that is being and will be designed for classroom use. The latter, while it will continue to include programs to be used by individual students to develop specific skills, will increasingly incorporate material or concepts to be utilized by groups of students simultaneously. It will be developed with courseware that will maximize its potential by providing a more total learning experience, which can and must be guided by trained teachers. It will be most effective in an environment infused with the personal motivation, guidance, encouragement, and interaction with teachers and other students. Finally, if nothing else convinces skeptics about the resistance of the school market to the threat of the home market, the lack of self-discipline characteristic of young people should be a sufficient indicator of the lack of success of a sustained attempt at home education.

For the sake of discussion, however, let us imagine that the commercial software producers find the home market so much more lucrative than the school market that the latter is abandoned. In that case, we still have the nonprofit software developers such as MECC, who have already established a good record for producing quality educational software at affordable prices. In fact, because they do offer educationally sound software at a fraction of the cost of commercially developed programs, it is possible if not probable that non-profit corporations could do what the home market alone can not do: run the commercial producers out of the school market. This remote but not entirely hypothetical possibility will become even more distant when producers begin to lower dramatically their prices and negotiate affordable price structures for multiple-copy purchases.

It seems probable that commercial software producers are here to stay, especially given recent expansion into software production by major publishers of textbooks and other educational materials. We may expect to see those commercial producers offering instructional programs designed for use by the largest number of students. Programs in basic reading, writing, and computational skills, as well as some of the more common social studies and science topics, will undoubtedly meet the needs of "typical" students. But commercial producers are less likely to invest the money to create software for more specialized topics or for special—especially handicapped—students. These narrower markets hold less potential for a return on their investments, and therefore we may see the nonprofit software developers filling the niches created by students with unique or special needs and interests. However, whether the relationship between commercial and nonprofit software producers will be complementary or competitive—or even both—is one of the many exciting enigmas surrounding the infancy of the computer in our schools.

REDEFINING THE PROBLEM

Instructional software for schools is here to stay—in spite of currently mediocre quality, in spite of piracy, in spite of the vast market for instructional software to be used in the home. These threats to the future of educational software are serious, but not likely to be fatal. The piracy and quality factors, as established earlier, will diminish with the maturing of the enterprise. The quality of software will improve with experience and increased involvement of educators in its design and development; and piracy can be expected to abate somewhat as educators become more aware of the legal and educational implications of illegal copying and as commercial software developers respond to market pressures for negotiation of more affordable prices and more flexible conditions in the use of purchased software. Even if success in the home market accomplishes the most drastic scenario of driving commercial software producers out of the school market, nonprofit developers and producers of educational software should be able to meet the needs of the schools. Not only are there several firmly established and healthily growing firms in this nonprofit sector, but we can look for the growth of new firms in this field, perhaps affiliated with institutions of higher learning.

In short, when analysts, observers, or software producers speak of the potential demise of instructional software for the schools, what they are really projecting is the demise of *commercially produced* educational software for the schools. Whether that possibility is remote or realistic should concern educators because the presence and competition of commercial software producers can stimulate and sustain the continued development of diverse products for the varying needs of education. But whether educators and students will be choosing their software from among a variety of commercial and nonprofit firms, or whether the commercial producers will abandon or be driven from the school market, depends upon the success of educators and commercial producers in resolving some of the current problems threatening the future of commercial software.

For once, educators have reason to be optimistic about the eventual and successful resolution of a problem that now looms large: keeping the school market for educational software alive. It is likely that educators and commercial software producers will, in fact, achieve satisfactory containment of piracy through their mutual efforts, and that commercial software developers will achieve necessary improvements in the quality of their products. Yet in the unlikely event that these resolutions are not satisfactorily achieved, the schools can still expect to be provided with both the quantity and quality of desired software by the nonprofit sector. The real concern, then, should not be the *existence* of quality instructional software in the schools, but how well this software will be integrated into the learning environment and curriculum.

REFERENCES

Bell, Trudy. "Copying Computer Software for Educational Purposes: Is It Allowed?" *Personal Computing,* November 1983, pp. 236-242.

Berger, Carl. Presentation to 1983 National Association of Elementary School Principals (NAESP) National Fellows Program, Orlando, Fla., July 4, 1983.

Consumer Reports, November 1983, pp. 614-617.

Davis, Philip J. and Reuben Hersh. *The Mathematical Experience.* Boston: Houghton-Mifflin, 1981.

Dyer, Susan R. and Richard C. Forcier. "How To Pick Computer Software," *Instructional Innovator,* September 1982, pp. 38-40.

"Electronic University," *Washington Post,* September 13, 1983, p.1, col. 6, p.A7, col. 4.

The Elements of Computer Education. Office of Public Instruction, Helena, Montana, 1983..

FINAL REPORT of the National Commission on New Technological Uses of Copyrighted Works, Library of Congress, Washington, D.C., 1978.

Finkel, Leroy. "When Is a Pirate a Thief?" *Electronic Learning,* October 1983, pp. 26,28.

Hoover, Todd and Sandra Gould. "The Pirating of Computer Programs: A Survey of Software Producers," *Educational Technology,* October 1982, pp. 23-26.

Kleiman, Glenn, Mary M. Humphrey, Trudy Van Buskirk. "Evaluating Educational Software," *Creative Computing,* October 1981, pp. 85-90.

Kulik, James A. "Synthesis of Research on Computer-Based Instruction," *Educational Leadership,* September 1983, pp. 19-21.

Larson, Eric. "Stiffened Software-Copyright Protection By Court Isn't Expected to Thwart Pirates," *The Wall Street Journal,* September 6, 1983.

Letellier, Lauren T. "Copying Software: Crime In The Classroom?" *Electronic Leaning,* January/February 1982, pp. 42, 44, 51.

Microcomputer Data. Quality Education Data, Inc. Presentation to NAVA Materials Council. New Orleans, La., January, 1983.

Milgrim, Roger M. "Program Purloiners Doubly Deterred," *Datamation,* v.29, no.3, March 1983, pp. 158-163.

"Missing Computer Software," *Business Week,* September 1, 1983, pp. 46-53.

Mitgang, Lee. Associated Press release. (Published in *Peoria Journal-Star,* November 7, 1983.)

Nunes, Dan. "Software Piracy Robs the Users," *Washington Post,* May 16, 1983, "Washington Business" section, pp. 21,22.

O'Brien, Thomas C. "Five Essays on Computers in Education," *Phi Delta Kappan,* October 1983, pp.110-112.

Orlansky, Jesse. "Effectiveness of CAI: A Different Finding," *Electronic Learning,* September, 1983, pp. 58-60.

"Quality Software: How to Know When You've Found It!" *Electronic Learning,* Nov./Dec. 1981, pp.33-36.

Shaffer, Richard. "Software Makers Losing Sales To Influx of Program Pirates," *Wall Street Journal,* May 1, 1981, p. 27.

U.S. Congress, Senate Judiciary Committee, 94th Cong., 1st session, 1975, S. Rept. 473.

U.S. Congress, House Judiciary Committee, 94th Cong., 2d session, 1976, H. Rept. 1476. (Guidelines for Classroom Copying . . .)

INFORWORLD, September 5, 1983, p. 30.

Walker, Decker. "Reflections on the Educational Potential and Limitations of Microcomputers," *Phi Delta Kappan,* October 1983, pp.103-107.

Waters, Craig. "An Apple a Day," *Inc.,* August 1983, pp.51-54.

Weiner, Cheryl. "The Hidden Cost of Copyright Infringement," *Classroom Computer News,* July-August, 1981, p. 38.

White, Mary Alice. "Synthesis of Research on Electronic Learning," *Educational Leaderhip,* May 1983, pp. 13-15.

GLOSSARY

1. **Archival program copies.** One or more tape or disk copies of original software (the master copy) kept on file to substitute in the event of accident or loss of originally-purchased software.
2. **Authoring programs.** High-level software programs that enable instructors to construct educational programs within a predefined format. The instructor needs no knowledge of computer programming and merely enters text, questions, and answers in response to prompts from the computer.
3. **Bit copy program.** A utility that is relatively immune to anti-piracy devices. It copies computer programs one bit at a time.
4. **Booting up.** Loading computers with software. For multiple use, it can be done sequentially with a single master copy.
5. **CAI.** Computer-assisted instruction. Programed learning by computer.
6. **Computer-based education.** CAI plus a management and administration system that supports it.
7. **Copyright Act.** This 1976 Copyright Act, P.L. 94-533, includes the copyright regulation of materials used in education and training. It codified the concept of "fair use" of material for instructional purposes. A 1980 amendment, P.L. 96-517, expanded the Copyright Act to include instructional computer software.
8. **Courseware.** Instructional software, plus such supporting print and nonprint materials as audiovisual materials, worksheets, study guides, texts, and examinations. Generally combined into an instructional package for lesson, unit, or course.

9. **Downloading.** Loading software or data into a computer *from* another computer directly, by telephone linkage, or through satellites, optical fiber, or cable.
10. **Drill-and-practice.** Rote knowledge and skill development. Simple cognitive process of repetition of facts and regurgitation of information.
11. **Dumb terminals.** Terminals that link with computers to interact with programs, but that cannot perform independently.
12. **Fair use.** Legally acceptable forms of or purposes for copying computer programs or other copyright material for instructional purposes as noted in P.L. 94-553.
13. **Flowchart.** Sequential, step-by-step pattern of logic and instructions used to map initially a computer program.
14. **Hardware.** Computer machinery itself, as opposed to the "software" (i.e., instructions) that gives the computer its utility.
15. **Learning games.** Computer software games designed to teach knowledge or skills while entertaining user.
16. **Loading.** Inserting computer programs, usually on disk or tape, into the hardware to program a computer.
17. **Master copy.** The purchased copy of a computer program usually in disk or casette form belonging to the owner who purchased it.
18. **Menu format.** Listing of tasks, lessons, or interest areas from which computer user selects the one set of instructions to perform a desired or preferred function.
19. **Monitor.** The television-like screen (i.e., cathode ray tube) that visually presents a computer's output.
20. **Networking.** Linking together of computers by telephone, cable, optical fiber, or satellite to provide interchanges of information or sharing of a program.
21. **Nibble copy programs.** Computer programs designed to "crack" much of the scrambled or otherwise protected software, making it possible to copy that software.
22. **Pirating.** Unauthorized copying of copyrighted materials, especially copyrighted computer software. Stealing.
23. **Program.** The software that drives or instructs the computer. May be on tape or disk or actually built into the computer hardware. P.L. 96-517: "A set of statements or instructions to be used directly or indirectly in a computer in order to bring about a certain result."

24. **Prompts.** Cues in instructional programs to elicit intended user responses.
25. **Software.** Computer programs. Instructions that tell a computer what to do. See program.
26. **Spreads.** Graphic charts of information provided by computer either on monitor or on printouts. Most commonly, these are charts of financial information and interactions.
27. **Turnkey mode.** A computer configuration in which a program is ready to operate as soon as the machine is turned on.
28. **Tutorial programs.** Software that questions learners and evaluates learner responses to aid them in knowledge and skill development.
29. **Uploading.** Loading software or data from one computer *into* another computer or network by telephone linkage, through satellites, optical fiber, or cable.
30. **User-friendly.** The more a computer can understand a diversity of common language and vernacular instructions, the "friendlier" it is considered to be for users.

APPENDIX A

FAIR USE OF EDUCATIONAL SOFTWARE

DANIEL T. BROOKS, ESQ.*

"Take not from others to such an extent and in such a manner that you would be resentful if they so took from you."[1]

INTRODUCTION

The micro-computer business, generally, and the educational applications business, specifically, are booming.[2] In fact, those businesses are growing too fast.[3] Moreover, mass computer and software markets, including educational markets, are still pretty low. Booming business and new markets inevitably lead to overly high prices, too often shoddy merchandise, too often poor after-sale support, and diffused accountability due to unclear and constantly changing distribution channels.[4]

[1] McDonald, *Non-Infringing Uses,* 9 Bull. Cr. Soc'y 466, 467 (1962).

[2] Morin, *British Computer Company Takes a Risky Step Into the U.S. Market,* The Wall Street Jour., Sep. 7, 1983, at 33, col. 1.

[3] Larson and Wells, *Shaken Osborne Computer Seeking Suitor in the Face of Possible Failure,* The Wall Street Jour., Sep. 12, 1983, at 35, col. 14; and Davis, *Pioneer of Cheap Computers, Timex Now Finds Sales Dropping Sharply,* The Wall Street Jour., Aug. 16, 1983, at 35, col. 4.

[4] *See,* Emmett, *American Education: The Dead End Of The 80s,* 7 Personal Computing 96 (Aug. 1983).

Such difficulties compound the problems of educators struggling to bring computer literacy to clamoring parents and students at all levels of the educational system. Educators and school systems are wrestling with these difficulties and with the overwhelming investment in hardware, software and teacher training that is required. In some cases, they are repeating the mistakes of businessmen before them. "The strategy seems to be 'buy now, plan later.'"[5] They are forgetting that the hardware is just the tip of the investment-iceberg. Software, maintenance, and training are the name of the game.

One solution to the software availability problem is obvious. Copying computer programs back and forth between the processor's internal circuits, memory, and peripherals is the essence of using the programs. Copying and copies are also essential to facilitate debugging and later audits of what occurred. They are also necessary to protect users against system crashes and untold other adversities of computer life.

In short, copying and copies are essential, inexpensive and untroubling to effect. So much so, that it is not surprising the industry is still struggling with the ethics of doing so.[6] When one adds a noble purpose in doing so—education—educators of all stripes are doing so, pausing only slightly, if at all, to ask questions such as:

(1) "May the school buy one copy of a program and make ten, one for each student's machine?"

(2) "May a copy on the hard disk of a multi-user system be used by all students?"

(3) "May the library acquire and loan copies to students, and, if so, what is the library's (school's) liability if students make pirate copies for their own use?"

---

[5] Feinberg, *Computers Contribute Little To Education, Study Finds,* The Washington Post, Sept. 16, 1983, at 1; *also see*, 7 Pres. Comp. at 97 ("[E]ven with a $2.1 million investment in hardware, Broward County, Fla. schools were underutilizing their 900 Apple II computers because of the lack of instructors and instruction time for teachers, as well as the failure to allocate money for appropriate software."); *Missing Computer Software,* Business Week, Sept. 1, 1980; and Schatz, *Feds Find Software the Problem,* 27 Datamation 66 (Aug. 25, 1981).

[6] *See, Self Assessment Procedure IX,* 25 Communications of ACM, No. 3, Mar. 1982, at 181, 189 (In Part V, Panel Responses to Scenarios, a panel of industry participants varied widely on the ethics of several scenarios); Parker, *Ethical DP Behavior Requires Action Plan,* Computerworld, Aug. 16, 1982, at 39, col. 1; Blakeslee, *Should Computer Profession Have a Code of Ethics,* The Stanford Observer, Jan. 1978; and *Industry in No Rush to Adopt Code of Conduct,* Computerworld, Nov. 12, 1979, at 39, col. 1.

Nor are educators alone. Software Piracy—that's the perjorative label—is rampant in the micro-computer business.[7] Some readers may have heard the young man Sam Donaldson interviewed at the end of August on ABC's Nightline. The young man made no bones about his copying of programs for friends and others. He didn't pause over the ethics, much less the legality, of what he was admitting. He justified his actions on the basis of the high price of software and that all his friends were doing the same thing.

The fundamental question raised by all of this—how much copying may be done despite the copyright laws—is not new. Only its new clothes. Computes are new. Software is new. The question is not.

There is even a specific section in the 1976 Copyright Act addressing "fair use" of literary works, such as *Moby Dick* and computer programs. On its face, that section appears to authorize just what educators wish to do, prepare multiple copies for classroom use. It provides in part that:

> "fair use of a copyrighted work . . . for purposes such as . . . teaching (including multiple copies for classroom use) . . . is not an infringement of copyright."[8]

But be careful! The multiplicity of copies is not the problem where computer programs are concerned. The real question is "Of what may multiple copies be made?"

Another promising area of inquiry lies in the "computer programs" section of the 1976 Copyright Act.[9] It expressly authorizes copying of computer programs "as an essential step" in using them.

But there are some preliminaries to analyzing these Sections. Both raise *defenses* to actions for copyright infringement. Understanding them requires understanding some copyright basics. Moreover, the 1976 Act made some changes to the U.S. copyright system that may prove unexpected to newcomers to the area. To avoid surprises, it seems best to start with some copyright basics.

It is also advisable to be clear at the outset that discussion is focused only on copyright. Some micro-computer programs are made available under trade secret licenses. That is not the usual case, but it is not

[7] Rosenbaum, *Software Piracy: Formulating A Plan for Protection,* Computerworld, Sept. 12, 1983, at 149, col. 1; and *See*, Shannon, *Copycatting in the Software Patch,* The New York Times, May 9, 1982, at 17, col. 1.

[8] 17 U.S.C. § 107.

[9] 17 U.S.C. § 117.

uncommon. There is no fair use concept in state trade secret law. As a general rule, there you may do only what the license agreement says, no more.

BASICS UNDER THE NEW COPYRIGHT ACT

Copyright Is Now AUTOMATIC in MOST Computer Programs.

Most computer programs are prepared in well known steps which proceed from conception, through flow charting, coding, compilation, testing and debugging, to production, distribution, maintenance and enhancement. At many stages, an expression of the program is "fixed in a tangible medium" from which it can be "perceived, reproduced or otherwise communicated for a period of more than transitory duration." Congress specifically contemplated that computer programs, once so fixed, would be protected by copyright as one of many kinds of literary works.[10]

Most programs have been so fixed by the time they are written on "coding sheets." Even programs being entered at terminals meet the simple test for fixation. Program code will almost invariably be permanently stored somewhere on tape or on disk for later editing or use.[11]

At the first instant of being so fixed, copyright in that expression *automatically* "subsists," whether or not the author(s) want it.[12] That is a significant change from prior law under which Federal copyright was elective and obtained by publication of the work with the familiar form of copyright notice affixed. Under the new system, the automatic copyright may be lost if certain things are done, *e.g.*, publication of the work without notice and without timely corrective action.[13] But, the initial vesting of copyright is automatic.

Registration of copyright is now the elective element of protection.[14] There are certain incentives to doing so, but registration is not mandatory. For example, registration is a precondition to suing on the

[10] 17 U.S.C. § 102(a) and § 101; and U.S. Cong., House Judiciary Committee, 94th Cong., 2d Sess., 1976, H.R. Rep. No. 941476 ("House Report"), at 54.

[11] *See, Apple Computer, Inc. v. Franklin Computer Corp.*, Dkt. Nos. 82-1582 and 82-1532 (3d Cir. Aug. 30, 1983). and *Williams Electronics, Inc. v. Artic International Inc.*, 685 F.2d. 870 (3d Cir. 1982).

[12] 17 U.S.C. 102(a).

[13] 17 U.S.C. § 405.

[14] 17 U.S.C. § 408.

copyright.[15] To collect statutory damages for infringement (from $250 to $10,000 per infringement) and attorney's fees, registration must have occurred before the infringement of unpublished works and within three months after first publication as to other works.[16] The registration certificate is also *prima facie* evidence of the validity of the copyright and of the facts stated if registration occurs within five years of first publication.[17]

Note that UNPUBLISHED works in which registered copyrights subsist are clearly contemplated under the new system. That is significant as to computer programs in particular due to industry practice of registering the program copyrights, but treating the so-called "source codes" as unpublished trade secrets. An encrypted form of the programs, the object code versions—*i.e.*, the "1's" and "0's" on the disks—are what is published. The notion is that like the formula for Coca-Cola, the trade secrets in the source code are safe because of the difficulty of discovering them by reverse-engineering the object code. Yet, just in case the secrets are not safe, there is perfected copyright in both the source and object code versions of the programs.

What Is Copyright?

At the instant a work is first fixed, the copyright owner is possessed of the five so-called "exclusive" rights in the work.[18] Those are the rights to:

(1) reproduce the work in copies (*e.g.*, to copy the work);
(2) prepare derivative works (*e.g.*, to adapt or transform the work);
(3) distribute copies of the work to the public (*e.g.*, to market copies);
(4) perform the work publicly (*e.g.*, to play video-games in arcades); and
(5) display the work publicly (*e.g.*, to hold up program listings at seminars).[19]

Collectively, these rights are known as "copyright." They are "exclusive" rights because only the copyright owner, someone authorized by the owner, or someone within an exception in the Act may do them.

[15] 17 U.S.C. § 411.
[16] 17 U.S.C. § 412.
[17] 17 U.S.C. § 411(c).
[18] 17 U.S.C. § 201 and § 101.
[19] 17 U.S.C. § 106.

As a consequence of the foregoing exclusive rights and the automatic subsistence of copyright in most programs, only the above three classes of persons—(1) the copyright owner, (2) someone authorized by the owner, or (3) someone authorized by the Act—may prepare duplicate disks, load programs from disks, cause computers to create additional copies within their memories, prepare working and archives copies, alter the functioning of programs, modify program code to run on particular computers, exhibit copies of program code to students and run programs in class. All these acts involve one or more of the above exclusive rights.

For example, to function, computers must copy. They move code from disk to memory, from memory to registers, etc. That involves reproducing the work in copies.[20] To debug code during class, the code must be printed-out or displayed in the "public" classroom. That involves reproducing the work in copies and/or displaying the work publicly.[21] Indeed, although this may sound a bit silly, running programs in class probably involves performance in the public classroom. Unrelated persons are present and watching as the programs go about producing results on the CRT or printer. It's like running a video tape in the classroom. It's just that computers are creating the displays.

Modifying the program code, say, to install Wordstar to run on your CRT and printer, involves one of three things. If there is little or no additional authorship, there probably is a reproduction of the work in copies.

---

[20] "Copies are material objects . . . in which a work is fixed by any method now known or later developed, and from which the work can be perceived, reproduced, or otherwise communicated either directly or with the aid of a machine or device." 17 U.S.C. § 101.

If loading programs and internal paging, etc. were not reproducing programs in copies, much of the *raison d'etre* behind present § 117 would be removed. *See, Final Report of the National Commission on New Technological Uses of Copyrighted Works,* Jul. 31, 1978, at 39.

Note the ambiguity in the word copies. *All* tangible embodiments of the work are copies, not just ones reproduced from other tangible embodiments. Thus, originals are also copies. Where important to the meaning of what is said in this article, an effort has been made to distinguish reproductions from originals, but the reader should be alert to the possibility of confusion.

[21] "To perform or display a work publicly means—(1) to perform or display it at a place open to the public or at any place where a substantial number of persons outside of a normal circle of a family and its social acquaintances are gathered . . . " 17 U.S.C. § 101.

If "new" authorship is introduced then there are either (1) derivative works[22] or (2) compilations.[23] Tinkering with program code, say, to make programs execute faster, probably involves derivative works. Distinct, "wrap-around," modifications that retain independent identities, probably involve compilations. For example, new sub-routines and drivers for new peripherals are typically prepared and "assembled" separately from the programs of which they are to become parts. They are linked to those programs in later steps. Thus, the sub-routines and drivers, and copyright in them, preexist the combination of them with the other programs. Thus, the combinations are compilations.

Ownership and Transfer of Copyrights and Exclusive Rights.

Under the new Copyright Act, copyright automatically subsists and generally "vests initially in the author or authors of the work."[24] Thus, subject to the "works made for hire" discussion to follow, teachers and students own the automatic copyrights in the programs they write.

Copyright (and any one or more of the exclusive rights) can only be acquired by others, not the actual authors, by transfers from the author(s). In employer-employee situations the transfers will usually be by operation of law under the "works made for hire" doctrine discussed below. In other cases, agreements or licenses are required.

Writings are mandatory for transfers of copyright (and any exclusive rights) unless the transfers are by operation of law.[25] Moreover, recording transfers at the Copyright Office is a precondition to suit for infringement. It is also advisable to cut off potentially superior rights of later transferees should the author(s) transfer the same program more

---

[22] A derivative work is one "based upon one or more preexisting works, such as a translation, . . . abridgement, condensation, or any other form in which a work may be recast, transformed, or adapted." 17 U.S.C. § 101.

[23] A compilation is "a work formed by the collection and assembling of preexisting materials or of data that are selected, coordinated, or arranged in such a way that the resulting work as a whole constitutes and original work of authorship. The term 'compilation' includes collective works." 17 U.S.C. § 101.

[24] 17 U.S.C. § 201(a). The ownership discussion will be somewhat more extensive than necessary to discuss fair use. Automatic copyright introduces complications for commercial employers and employees that created problems. Teachers and schools needn't repeat unpleasant commercial experience if warned in time.

[25] 17 U.S.C. § 204(a).

than once.[26] In short, *written agreements* are essentially mandatory when addressing copyright matters.

Takers of copyrights by transfer should be aware that transfers from individual authors cannot be for the full term of copyright. To protect authors from over-bearing publishers, under 17 U.S.C. § 203, 35 years after grant, and for a period of five years, authors have a non-waivable right to reclaim copyrights in their works. Since the expected useful life of most programs is less than 35 years, that right is probably not substantial in most situations.

Joint Works.

Particularly for large programs, there may be more than one author in which copyright initially vests under § 201(a). Large jobs are often broken down into separate programs or sub-routines assigned to separate groups. Co-authors of "joint works" are tenants-in-common. All may use the whole work, but must account to the other co-authors.[27]

Joint works must be distinguished from "compilations." The former arise when the authors intend *at the time of writing* that the separate portions be merged into a single work.[28] The latter consist of a "collection and assembling of *preexisting* materials."[29] There is a single, jointly owned copyright in joint works. In effect, two copyrights exist in compilations, one in the compilation itself and another in each of the constituent works. The authors of contributions to an encyclopedia are free to use their works, just not the precise fixations of them which the encyclopedia publisher has produced.[30]

Thus, depending on the authors' intentions at the time of writing, works of multiple employees and/or consultants on sub-routines of a single application package result in one of two situations: (1) many owners of the copyright in the single, but jointly owned, application package or (2) separately copyrighted contributions to the application package in which a compilation-copyright in the aggregate may lie elsewhere.

[26] 17 U.S.C. § 205(d) & (e).

[27] House Report at 121.

[28] 17 U.S.C. § 101; House Report at 121.

[29] 17 U.S.C. § 101 (emphasis added); note 23, *supra*.

[30] *See, e.g.*, 17 U.S.C. § 201(c) dealing with the lesser included category "collective works".

That result raises interesting possibilities. Take, for example, the package of utilities included with OS/370. They may or may not have been prepared by consultants to IBM contemplating a joint work. If they were, the consultant-authors of one of the parts may use the whole package at Amdahl. However, there is a duty to account to the other co-authors for all use.

If the utilities were not prepared contemplating a joint work, only the one part may be used in other employment by its consultant-authors. Yet, they need not account for that use.

Works Made For Hire.

Under the "works made for hire" doctrine, employers automatically become the "authors" for purposes of the Act.[31] Indeed, employers and employees must expressly agree "otherwise *in a written instrument*" to change the statutory result.[32]

The "works made for hire" section codifies prior decisional law which therefore remains valuable in interpreting it.[33] Note that where multiple consultants and employees have common employers, the "works made for hire" doctrine simplifies matters by usually creating one author, the common employers. Whether or not the programs are joint works, compilations, etc. is of much less significance where all rights are vested in one "author-employer."

Works made for hire come about in two ways. First, there are works by "employees" acting "within the scope" of their employment.[34] The touchstones here are familiar to lawyers. They are the agency questions of (1) the employer's "right to direct and supervise the manner in which the work was being performed," (2) "at whose insistence,

[31] 17 U.S.C. § 201(b).

[32] 17 U.S.C. § 201(b) (emphasis added).

[33] House Report at 121. These cases must be cautiously analyzed. Copyright is now automatic. Drafts, working papers and other documents essential to the operation of many enterprises are now copyrighted. Previously, it was not necessary to address ownership of copyright in such works unless someone sought federal copyright. Now it is. Unexpected results may lead to "new law" to correct perceived inequities.

Many commercial enterprises have been caught in unexpected controversies with employees. School systems may likewise be taken by surprise. That is the principal reason for expanding this ownership discussion beyond what is strictly necessary to discuss fair use.

[34] 17 U.S.C. § 101.

expense, time and facilities the work was created," and (3) "the nature and amount of compensation."[35]

There is considerable subtlety in those familiar issues. Although the statute requires employees, not employers, to seek written agreements to alter the statutory presumption, employers may find written agreements with employees desirable. They can clarify the "scope of employment" and make appropriate provision for works arguably outside that scope. They also can address corresponding trade secret ownership issues that are beyond the scope of this copyright article.

Programs written during school hours, in the classroom, with school computers and disks seem pretty clearly within the scope and course of the teacher's employment. Yet such factors are not necessarily determinative. English teachers writing VisiCalcs for their own purposes, not as part of class exercises or preparation, may be outside the scope of their employment. How about programs written at home on their own computers?

The broader the assigned tasks, position, authority and discretion of teachers and employees, the stronger the employers' position vis a vis ownership of such off-hour programs. But VisiCalcs aren't the property of GMs just because their chief financial executives used their home-based Apples to create them. Nor are networking programs the property of school systems just because teachers wrote them. Suppose the programs clearly are not related to any current or contemplated school-business. Such ambiguities may be clarified somewhat by express agreements, even though they are not strictly necessary.

Second, there are so-called "specially commissioned works" made for hire. Works authored by consultants and other independent contractors may become "works made for hire . . . if the parties expressly [so] agree *in a written instrument*."[36]

Consultants and third party supplies are common in the computer industry. The latter increasingly so in recent years. Whatever the scope of employment, even individuals acting as software suppliers are virtually never employees. Consultants may or may not be employees depending on circumstances.

Some teachers may not be employees and may own the copyrights in their programs for that reason. Temporaries and substitutes are not

[35] *Scherr v. Universal Match Corp.*, 417 F.2d 497, 500, 164 U.S.P.Q. 225 (2d Cir., 1969).

[36] 17 U.S.C. § 101 (emphasis added).

uncommon. Many are employees assigned to floating responsibility. But others are independent contractors. FICA and other fringe benefits are saved by the school system through that status. As independent contractors, they own their programs. It may not be very fair to the school system in some situations, but that is the result.

The result is the same in the commercial case. When users pay consultants or independent software organizations on a "cost plus" or even a "time and materials" basis to custom prepare new programs tailored to the users' needs, there is a clear basis for the users to seek copyright ownership. The authors took little development risk in the transactions. The authors' rights to reuse their work should involve royalties to the risk-bearing developer-users.

But that is not the result under the Copyright Act. Section 201 is explicit. There may be implied-in-fact licenses and/or express oral licenses for the employers to use the copies of the programs they bought and paid for, but there is no ownership of the copyrights.

On the other hand, that may not be as unfair as it sounds in many cases. Many custom programming jobs involve changes to conform preexisting packages to the particular user's needs. Others involve the vendors' expertise in some vertical market such as banking applications. They likely also involve kernels of code previously written for similar purposes. User-ownership of copyright in minor patches to preexisting packages, or to such kernels, no matter what the agreed price, is almost never appropriate. the supplier's right to modify the preexisting package for other customers, reuse the kernels, license the patches to others, etc. is at stake. Without such patches and kernels there is no real expertise and the whole package is less marketable. Moreover, unless such kernels are reusable, users are constantly paying to reinvent the wheel. The supplier has to be able to price the job counting on reusing the kernels and patches elsewhere.

Thus, the automatic copyrights in programs and sub-routines prepared by non-employees are the property of the employer-users only if there are writings under which they are either (1) within the specially commissioned "works made for hire" section or (2) conveyed or exclusively licensed.

Only certain limited classes of works are eligible to become "specially ordered or commissioned" works. The works must be for use (1) as a contribution to a collective work, . . . (2) as a translation, (3) as a supplementary work, (4) as a compilation, or (5) as an instructional text."[37] These categories are likely to be narrowly construed and are not likely to be expandable by agreement.[38] Note, for example, that joint works and derivative works do not qualify as such. They must also be "contributions to a collective work," etc.

To be eligible as specially commissioned works, programs and subroutines must also be "translations" (*e.g.*, rewrites from COBOL to Fortran), "supplementary works" (*e.g.*, program enhancements or documentation of existing programs), or "instructional texts" (*e.g.*, self-help programs, program documentation and user's and operator's manuals). Any of these could become "works made for hire" under an appropriate written agreement to that effect.

However, usual, stand-alone programs and subroutines for specific purposes, not designed to be included within larger programs, would not come within these specially commissioned works classifications. Such programs would not be, *and could not by agreement be made to become,* "works made for hire" of which employers become the "authors" by operation of law.[39]

Note that under the "works made for hire" doctrine, in the absence of contrary written agreements, employers, not employees, own program copyrights. Thus, school systems, not teachers, likely own the copyrights in programs written by teachers on the job. BUT, the reverse is true in the case of non-employees. They, not their employers, own program copyrights. Thus, students and non-employee substitute teachers likely own their own product, whether in class or otherwise.

COMPUTER USES OF COPYRIGHTED WORKS

Distinguish Copyrights from Copies.

The ownership referred to above is of the copyrights and the individual exclusive rights. Ownership of particular *copies* is a separate matter.[40] Be careful to distinguish the original expression and literary

---

[37] 17 U.S.C. § 101.

[38] They reflect careful balancing by Congress of competing interests of authors and producers in the movie and recording industries. House Report at 121. Moreover, significant factors, *e.g.*, the term of protection for the work, turn on the works made for hire classification. Such matters are unlikely to be determined to be variable by private agreement.

[39] House Report at 121.

[40] 17 U.S.C. § 202.

property in Melville's original manuscript from each copy of *Moby Dick*.

Computer Use—Section 117.

The distinction can be critical. *Owners* of copies that have been lawfully made have certain statutory rights such as to sell the copies and to display them publicly.[41] Specifically in the case of computer programs, Section 117 of the Act provides that:

> "Notwithstanding the provisions of [the section setting forth the 5 exclusive rights], it is not an infringement for the owner of a *copy* of a computer program to make or authorize the making of another *copy or adaptation* of that computer program provided:
>
> (1) that such a new copy or adaptation is created as *an essential step* in the utilization of *the computer program* in conjunction with a machine and that it is used in no other manner, or
>
> (2) that such new copy or adaptation is for *archival purposes only* and all archival copies are destroyed in the event that continued possession of the computer program should cease to be rightful.
>
> Any exact copies prepared in accordance with the provisions of this section may be leased, sold, or otherwise transferred, along with the copy from which such copies were prepared, only as part of the lease, sale, or other transfer of all rights in the program. Adaptations so prepared may be transferred only with the authorization of the copyright owner."[42]

Note that Section 117 applies only to owned copies and that it expressly contemplates transfer of the original *and* all reproductions to others. Lessees and borrowers of copies may only copy and adapt as authorized in their leases and loan agreements. Moreover, adaptations may only be transferred with the copyright owner's consent. "Adaptations" are a lesser included category of "derivative works." Thus, the tinkerings with programs discussed above may only be transferred with the consent of the owners of copyright in the underlying programs. The "wrap-around" sub-routines, however, are independent works which, by themselves, may be transferred as their authors see fit.

The clear purport of this Section is to authorize disk to core to

[41] 17 U.S.C. § 109.

[42] 17 U.S.C. § 117 (emphasis added).

register, etc. copying, and back-up copying, as necessary to use computer programs. The Section also makes clear that transferring *everything* is as legitimate as destroying all the clones, transferring the original under the authority of Section 109, and having the transferee create new copies under Section 117.

Note that proliferation of users of the same original—*i.e.,* making copies for transfer while keeping some for your own use—is thus the proscribed act, not mere copying. Indeed, Section 117 doesn't even restrict reproduction to the owned original. The "program," not just the owned copy of it, may be copied and adapted. Thus, the Section seems to authorize reproducing the program from originals owned by others just as long as another copy of the same program is owned by the person doing the reproducing. The same result seems appropriate on a "no harm, no foul" theory. The copyright owner has sold copies to everybody. There is just some borrowing going on that does not reduce revenues.

Also note that the Section speaks to only 2 of the 5 exclusive rights—adaptating and copying. It does not speak to the other 3 exclusive rights—distributing copies to the public, performing the work publicly, and displaying the work publicly. Thus, to the extent those 3 things are necessary to use the program, either those acts must be determined to be within the implied scope of the license to use the programs or analysis must proceed under the "fair use" Section, not Section 117.

Most Over-the-Counter Software Transactions Are Sales of Copies.

In the educational software and other micro-computer software markets, most transactions are tantamount to sales of the copies to the users. For example, even in the main-frame market, custom and prepackaged software is often available for a one-time fee for substantially its entire useful life. Periodic fees, if any, are for future services rendered, such as program maintenance and enhancements, not ongoing use. Back-up copies on media to be owned by users, not the vendors, are contemplated. Indeed, the original copy may be delivered via user-owned media supplied to the vendor for that purpose.

In the mass market for micro-computers and software, the "sale" aspects of transactions are even more clear. One-time fees are the rule, with little if any on-going support promised, even for additional consideration. Some packages include license forms which purport to bind the user upon breaking the seal or shrink-wrap and which by their terms detract from characterizing the transaction as a sale, but the efficacy of these has not been proven.

In short, most program licenses look like sales, and are economically the equivalent of sales, at least of the copies. Restrictions on use and disposition of property after sale have always met with some judicial skepticism as possibly "unreasonable restraints on alienation."[43] That skepticism would seem reinforced by the express terms of Section 109 and 117, among others, of the Copyright Act. Ownership of copies carries certain intrinsic user rights mentioned above.

Finally, many vendor licenses are ambiguous regarding title to the copies. They speak of licensing—the intellectual property notion—not leasing—the tangible property notion. Although no cases have been found on this precise point, it seems likely that such ambiguities in vendor-prepared forms will be resolved against vendors, leaving users with title, at least to the copies. That would leave the users free to ignore the traditional license restrictions on user-copying, on user-modifications, on user-resales, or off-premises archiving, etc. to the extent necessary to use the programs as authorized by Section 117.

Fortunately for program proprietors, it does not follow from mere sales of copies that their copyrights have been transferred to users. Under 17 U.S.C. § 202, sales of copies are not sales of copyrights, and vice versa.

FAIR USE OF COMPUTER PROGRAMS

So-called "fair use" is an aged judicially developed defense to an action for copyright infringement. It is justified "to avoid rigid application of the copyright statute when, on occasion, it would stifle the very creativity which that law is designed to foster."[44] The doctrine has been described as "entirely equitable and . . . so flexible as virtually to defy definition."[45]

It is a defense to copyright infringement. Thus, plaintiff has already

---

[43] *Cf., Blazon, Inc. v. DeLuxe Game Corp.*, 268 F. Supp. 416 (S.D. N.Y. 1965) and *Platt & Munk Co. v. Republic Graphics, Inc.*, 315 F.2d 847 (2d Cir. 1963).

[44] *Iowa St. Univ. Research Foundation, Inc. v. American Broadcasting Cos.*, 621 F.2d 57 (2d Cir. 1980).

[45] *Time, Inc. v. Bernard Geis Assoc.*, 293 F. Supp. 130 (S.D. N.Y. 1968).

established or is likely to establish copyright ownership and unauthorized copying, preparing of derivatives works, distribution of copies to the public, public performance, and/or public display. It is also likely that defendant has failed or will fail to make out other defenses such as a license, an assignment or joint ownership of the work in question.

Fair Use—Section 107.

For the first time, the 1976 Copyright Act codifies the doctrine of "fair use."

> "Notwithstanding the provisions of [the section setting forth the 5 exclusive rights], the fair use of a copyrighted work, including such use by reproduction in copies . . . or by any other means specified by that section, for purposes such as criticism, comment, news reporting, *teaching (including multiple copies for classroom use), scholarship,* or *research,* is not an infringement of copyright. In determining whether the use made of a work in any particular case is a fair use the factors to be considered shall include—
>
> (1) the purpose and character of the use, including whether such use is of a commercial nature or is for *nonprofit educational purposes*;
>
> (2) the nature of the copyrighted work;
>
> (3) the amount and substantiality of the portion used in relation to the copyrighted work as a whole; and
>
> (4) the effect of the use upon the potential market for or value of the copyrighted work."[46]

That Section was specifically enacted by Congress to "restate the present judicial doctrine of fair use, not to change, narrow, or enlarge it in any way."[47] Thus, as was the case with the works made for hire doctrine, prior decisions remain valuable in interpreting the new Section.

It is significant that "fair use" is a defense whether or not you "own" the copy. Indeed, the Section speaks of the fair use of the work, not any particular copy or copies. It is also significant that the Section affords a defense to allegations of infringement of any of the 5 exclusive rights. Section 107 differs from Section 117 in both these respects.

---

[46] 17 U.S.C. § 107 (emphasis added).

[47] House Report at 66.

Reflects Intensive Congressional Concern with Educational Arguments for Broader Rights.

However, it is also clear that as early as 1967, in considering copyright law reform, Congress carefully considered and explicitly rejected arguments by educators and others for broader exemptions for educational uses of copyrighted works.

> "*Intention as to classroom reproduction*
> Although the works and uses to which the doctrine of fair use is applicable are as broad as the copyright law itself, most of the discussion of section 107 has centered around questions of classroom reproduction, particularly photocopying. The arguments on the question are summarized at pp. 30–31 of this Committee's 1967 report (H.R. Rep. No. 83, 90th Cong. 1st Sess.), and have not changed materially in the intervening years.
> The Committee also adheres to its earlier conclusion, that a 'specific exemption freeing certain reproductions of copyrighted works for educational and scholarly purposes from copyright control is not justified.'"[48]

Thus, section 107 represents a careful balance of the rights of copyright proprietors against the need of educators and students for use of copyrighted materials. Although the doctrine may be fuzzy, it is clearly applicable to, and restricts the copying permissible for, classroom use. The noble aims of education afford no blanket exemption from the copyright laws.

Purpose and Character of the Use.

The Section sets out four areas of inquiry. The list is expressly not exhaustive. First is the purpose and character of the use.

Educational uses are precisely the kind for which the "purpose factor" was intended to weigh favorably. But, "a finding of nonprofit educational purpose does not automatically compel a finding of fair use."[49]

Moreover, there is a "same function test" weighing against fair use of works originally created for the very purposes for which they were copied.[50] Educational software is therefore less susceptible to copying

[48] House Report at 66–67.

[49] *Marcus v. Rowley,* 695 F.2d 1171, 1175 (9th Cir. 1983).

[50] *Iowa St. Univ. Research Foundation, Inc. v. American Broadcasting Cos.,* 621 F.2d 57 (2d Cir. 1980).

for educational purposes than other software. That is, after all, consistent with the notion that copyright is to encourage creativity. Unfettered copying of works created for educational purposes discourages creation of other educational works. As noted by the Judiciary Committee in 1967:

> "Textbooks and other material prepared primarily for the school market would be less susceptible to reproduction for classroom use than material prepared for general public distribution."[51]

Thus, as to educational software, *i.e.*, software prepared primarily for the school market, this factor is not as helpful as might first appear. It is certainly not enough by itself to assure a finding of fair use.

Nature of the Work.

The next factor is the nature of the copyrighted work. In addressing this factor, courts have distinguished creative works such as art and fiction from informative works such as anthologies and directories. "[T]he scope of fair use is greater when informational type works, as opposed to more creative products, are involved."[52]

Educational software can be either creative or informational. Many, indeed most, computer programs are the result of the application of known and relatively ordinary programming skills to solving particular problems. Thus, they involve little, if any, creativity in the sense of bells ringing and lights going on. Some may rise to that level of creativity, but most do not.

Thus, in most cases, educational software is susceptible to fair use under this factor.

Amount and Substantiality of the Portion Used.

The third factor, the amount and substantiality of the use, is highly troublesome as applied to software.

There are quantitative—how much was copied—and qualitative—the importance to the work of what was copied—tests in this factor. First, as to the quanitative part, few entertain the notion that *the*

---

[51] U.S. Congress, House Judiciary Committee, 90th Cong., 1st Sess., 1967, H.R. Rep. No. 90-83 ("1967 House Report"), at 34.

[52] *Universal City Studios, Inc. v. Sony Corp.*, 659 F.2d 963, 972 (9th Cir. 1981), *cert. granted,* 102 S.Ct. 2926 (1982).

entirety of Herman Melville's classic could be put on a Xerox machine and freely passed from school to student, and student to student. Yet, when it comes to another form of literary work—computer programs—that is precisely what people do.

Software is different from novels, essays, etc. Excerpts of great novels are probably enough to teach English and Melville's genius. Excerpts of computer programs may be enough to illustrate good programming techniques, the differences between source and object code, etc. But that isn't the real concern. Copies for students to use on their computers are the issue.

To be useable, computer programs must be copied virtually in their entirety. A few instructions may have to be changed, but 99% MUST be the same or they won't work. Copying so much of a work has never been contemplated as "fair use." Thus the quantitative test almost always mitigates against fair use.

As to software, that is also true of the qualitative test. Indeed, the copying of programs is so complete that the two aspects of the test merge. The whole work, including its important parts, must be copied.

Where the alleged infringement is not copying of the whole work for use with a computer, the two aspects of this factor retain their identity and meaning. Teachers might print the code to illustrate points in programming classes or prepare derivative works for the same purpose. If the printout is of the BIOS of the operating system to show students what device drivers look like, that is likely not much code, but it is very important code. The BIOS is the device-dependent code critical to the manufacturer's product and its identity. The "not much" conclusion suggests fair use while the "important part" suggests less fair use than if another portion of code had been used.

However, as noted above, in copying-for-use cases, the quantitative and qualitative tests amount to the same thing. In either case, copying of whole works is outside the contemplation of fair use for all but very short works. For example, Congress only contemplated that there would be fair use under section 107 for "reproduction by a teacher or student of *a small part* of a work to illustrate a lesson."[53] That is entirely consistent with cases on the subject.

For example, in the recent cases of *Marcus v. Rowley*,[54] "almost 50% of defendant's [Learning Activity Package] was a verbatim copy of

---

[53] House Report of 65 (emphasis added).

[54] 695 F.2d 1171, 1177 (9th Cir. 1983).

plaintiff's [Cake Decorating Made Easy] booklet and that 50% contained virtually all of the substance of the defendant's book. . . . Defendant's LAP could have been a photocopy of plaintiff's booklet but for the fact that defendant retyped plaintiff's material." That was enough despite the fact that only 15 infringing copies were made and neither the defendant nor the school district she taught for derived any profit from the LAP. As the court stated, "this court has long maintained the view that wholesale copying of copyrighted material precludes application of the fair use doctrine."[55]

In short, even though for non-commercial, educational purposes, the copying of entire works is too excessive for the fair use defense to apply.[56]

Market Effect.

The final factor listed in Section 107 is the effect of the use upon the potential market for or value of the copyrighted work. In essence, "a use which supplants any part of the normal market for a copyrighted work would ordinarily be considered an infringement."[57]

It has also been said that this is the most important factor, although it "must almost always be judged in conjunction with the other three criteria."[58] In *Marcus v. Rowley,* the appeals court was faced with a lower court finding that "it was unable to conclude that the defendant's copying had any effect on the market for the plaintiff's booklet."[59] Frankly, that finding was probably wrong in that two home economics teachers in the same area probably have highly overlapping markets of highly limited size. Thus 15 copies used by some 60 or so of the defendant's students was likely a severe dent in plaintiff's total market. However, the appeals court did not reverse the finding of fact. Instead it held that "The mere absence of measurable pecuniary damage does not require a finding of fair use. . . . Fair use is to be determined by a consideration of all of the evidence in the case. . . . Thus, despite the

[55] Id. at 1176.

[56] *See, Encyclopaedia Britannica Educational Corp. v. Crooks,* 447 F. Supp. 243, 251 (W.D. N.Y. 1978); *Quinto v. Legal Times of Washington, Inc.,* 506 F. Supp. 554, 560 (D. D.C. 1981).

[57] 1967 House Report at 35.

[58] Id.

[59] 695 F.2d at 1177.

trial court's finding, we conclude that the [other] factors analyzed weigh decisively in favor of the conclusion of no fair use."[60]

In short, strong enough cases on the character of use, the nature of the work and the substantiality of the copying will control this factor.

Print Media Guidelines.

Just in case the foregoing discussion leaves any doubt that "fair use" is not likely to be applicable to copying for classroom use of computer programs, especially educational programs, the guidelines negotiated by the Ad Hoc Committee of Educational Institutions and Organizations on Copyright Law Revision should be mentioned. These guidelines were (1) approvingly incorporated in the House Report on the bill which became the 1976 Copyright Act,[61] (2) adopted by the conference committee that reconciled the House and Senate versions of the bills,[62] (3) applied by the court in *Marcus v. Rowley*,[63] and (4) were expressly incorporated in the recent settlement of the action brought by publishers against a private photocopy center and NYU.[64] The guidelines deal only with printed works, as do the cases so far decided. Computers and clear applicability of the copyright laws to software are both too new for there to be reported decisions in this area.

The guidelines distinguish between (1) single copies for use by the teacher in preparing for or teaching classes and for scholarly research and (2) multiple copies (not to exceed the number of students in the course) for classroom use or discussion. In both cases, there are overriding prohibitions against copying as a "substitute for the purchase of books, publishers' reprints or periodicals;" against copying "directed by higher authority" than the teacher; and copying "repeated with respect to the same item by the same teacher from term to term."[65]

Limitations on the extent of copying are also clear in both cases. Teachers may only copy a chapter, article from a periodical or newspaper, short story, chart, etc. for their own use. Multiple copies for

[60] *Id.*

[61] House Report at 68–69.

[62] U.S. Congress, Conference Committee, 94th Cong., 2d Sess., 1976, Conf. Rep. No. 94-1733 ("Conference Report"), at 70.

[63] 695 F.2d at 1178–79.

[64] *See, Copying Center Comes To Terms With Publishers,* 26 P.T.C.J. 144, 145 (Jun. 9, 1983).

[65] House Report at 69.

classroom use must meet tests of brevity and spontaneity as well as the overriding limitations mentioned above.

Brevity requires that copies of poems not exceed 250 words or the whole poem if less than that. For prose it requires that copies not exceed 1,000 words or 10% of the work, whichever is less, or the whole work in *some* cases, *i.e.*, the whole article, story or essay if only 2,500 words or less. For so-called "special" works, usually for children, copies may not exceed 2 pages or 10% of the words.[66] Finally, there is a cumulative effect test that limits copying of all material to one course, not more than one work from the same author nor more than two from the same collective work or periodical, and not more than nine instances of multiple copying for one course during one term.[67]

These guidelines were strongly criticized by the American Association of University Professors and the Association of American Law Schools as too restrictive. Yet the House Judiciary Committee expressly rejected those criticisms and found "the guidelines are a reasonable interpretation of the minimum standards of fair use" apparently in the sense that they afforded teachers a safe harbor, not an exclusive statement of the scope of the fair use exception.[68]

The gist of the guidelines is clear. Copying the entirety of a work is very much the exception, not the rule, and then it is only permissible for short works and never as an institutional approach to supplying course materials. While the safe harbor nature of these guidelines means the door is open to judicial approval of more liberal copying, that door is not so wide open as to admit wholesale copying of entire works no matter how laudible the purpose.

APPLYING THE FAIR USE DOCTRINE TO EDUCATIONAL SOFTWARE

It is apparent that in enacting Section 107 of the 1976 Copyright Act, Congress considered and specifically rejected appeals for broader exemptions for non-profit educational uses of copyrighted works. It is also clear that the concept of fair use embodied in Section 107 is the historical one that may not even apply where copying is so extensive,

[66] House Report at 68–69.

[67] House Report at 69.

[68] House Report at 72.

as it must be if computer programs are to be used, as to amount to a copying of substantially all of the work. Many courts assert that the fair use doctrine is not even applicable to such total takings through copying.[69]

Thus, insofar as the question is the first one put at the outset of this paper—"May the school buy one copy of a program and make ten, one for each student's machine?"—the answer is painfully obviously in the negative. That is what leads to assertions such as "The only teachers who aren't copying software illegally are the ones who don't know how."[70]

However, the answers to the other two questions set forth above are not so negative. The first of these two questions involved the use of hard disks. Copying a program to hard disk from floppy disk is part of using it. To that extent it is impliedly within the license accompanying the shrink-wrapped package unless specifically excluded. Moreover, it is expressly authorized by Section 117 of the Copyright Act in the case of *owned* copies, which, as seen above, is most cases.

So far so good. However, use of that hard disk as a well from which each student's machine may draw water as needed probably crosses the bounds of permissible copying. On the other hand, because section 117 speaks of copying "the program" (once a copy of the program is owned), it appears the students could use the hard disk that way if the school bought copies for each student but chose to have them reproduce the one on the hard disk into their machines rather than work from their own floppy disks.

On the other hand, if only one original is acquired by the school, simultaneous use by the teacher and 30 students impermissibly expands the number of users of the original copy. Section 117 clearly contemplates transfer of reproductions to others *only with* the original. As a result, as noted in discussing that section above, Section 117 makes proliferating users, not copies, the offense.

However, the original copy may be an educational networking program, i.e., one that connects several TRS-80s together to form a single

---

[69] If there is any lingering doubt on this point, one need only refer to Professor Nimmer's treatise on copyright law § 13.05[d] where are collected a number of cases on exactly this point.

[70] *Computers: Living With Great Expectations,* Inside Education, Spring/Summer 1983, at 13, 16 (quoting Walter Koepke, a computer specialist for BOCES in Putnam-Northern Westchester, N.Y.)

system permitting teachers to monitor and/or control student activity at their TRS-80. If so, use for its intended purpose includes copying such portions of that program into each student's machine as necessary to serve the purpose. That is not so much a "fair use" question. It is a question of the implied scope of the license to use programs for their intended purpose.

In the case of owned copies, it is also a question of the scope of Section 117. That Section authorizes as many copies as are necessary to use "the program" with "a machine." It is at least arguable that the machine contemplated by Section 117, by the program's author and by the user-teacher encompasses the network of TRS-80s that the network program services. If so, such use is expressly encompassed within Section 117.

The interesting question arises when the unity of contemplation ceases. VisiCalc was designed as a single-user program. Thus, although the user-teacher may still contemplate the network of TRS-80s to be a single machine for the user-teacher's purposes, VisiCalc's authors do not share that view.

Whose view controls application of Section 117? That's not clear. But it is likely to be treated as a question of fact. Thus a school using a main-frame with so-called "dumb" terminals for each student is more likely to be using "a machine" than one using a network of computers of substantially equal intelligence at each node. There remains one machine even if the main-frame partitions its core into 64K banks, one for each "dumb" terminal, and loads into each bank one copy of the program. There really is only one machine.

In the latter case, it depends on one's viewpoint. There are several TRS-80s. But, the school, the owner of the first copy, is using "the program" with "a machine" (network probably acquired as a unit) in a manner at least not inconsistent with the manner in which the program was designed to be used.

In sum, using one copy of, say, VisiCalc to load the hard disk is permissible. If copies are purchased for each student-user, it also appears that they may use the hard disk as the source of working copies in their own machines. But, if there are not purchased copies for each student, permitting each student SIMULTANEOUSLY to have a local copy for use in that student's machine involves a prohibited proliferation of users of the same original copy of a program not intended to be used in that manner. But for the substantiality of the copying, there might be a fair use defense.

The key word, simultaneously, may have tipped another fruitful area of inquiry. COPIES of a work made by or under the authority of the owner of copyright are transferrable under Section 109 and 117 of the Copyright Act if they are owned by the transferor. As a result, SERIAL use of such copies is permissible. Coursework may require simultaneous use by the 30 students in the class. But only 30 copies are required if the next class uses the same copies. And, under Section 117, archive and back-up copies of each of the 30 are permissible, so destruction of working copies by careless students should not prove troublesome.

The school library may also acquire 30 copies and lend them to students. That is within Section 109. However, there is a lawsuit pending by several major software suppliers against the growing practice of doing just that commercially.[71] Frankly, unless software sales practices change materially, that suit is likely a loser. Sections 109 and 117 are quite explicit, as are years of history of what we may do with our copies of *Moby Dick*.

There is hope if these software suppliers can establish, as Universal tried to do in the Betamax case,[72] that the only, or substantially the only, purpose served by such leasing and lending of copies is facilitating illegal copying by the borrowers. Then there is "aiding and abetting" of the borrowers' illegal acts by the lender.[73]

However, as was the case in Betamax, that is not an easy demonstration to make. There are legitimate purposes served by such libraries.

---

[71] *Keep industry spat out of court*, InfoWorld, Sep. 5, 1983 at 30, col. 1.

[72] *Universal City Studios, Inc. v. Sony, Corp.*, 659 F.2d 963 (9th Cir. 1981), *cert. granted*, 102 S. Ct. 2929 (1982).

[73] Incidently, under Section 504(c) of the Copyright Act, there is some protection afforded to a librarian or other employee or agent of a nonprofit educational institution, library, or archives who infringes by reproducing the work in copies within the scope and course of his or her employment in the mistaken impression such copying was "fair use". In essence, the normal statutory damages, from $250 to $10,000 for each infringement, may not be awarded. If the plaintiff can prove actual damages, those may be collected. But as *Marcus v. Rowley* illustrates, that is not altogether easy.

Thus, back-up copies made by a prudent libraries before undertaking lending to students may not involve statutory damages when it is later demonstrated that students engaged in wholesale piracy of which the school had no knowledge up to that time.

Borrowers may be "trying before buying." Providing loan-copies for that purpose is perfectly legitimate and, indeed, constructive activity that the software suppliers may wish to encourage. Thus, the suit is by no means likely to succeed.

One final piece of practical advice. School systems and libraries often effect bulk purchases to obtain favorable prices. Software vendors might prove particularly receptive to such approaches. Piracy of all kinds is so prevalent that an honest approach of that sort stands a good chance of being encouraged.[74] Moreover, if the program is of general utility, not just a game, or limited to the educational market, the more students that become familiar with a product the more likely they are to become purchasers themselves or on behalf of later employers.[75] Such "seeding" of the market may permit the vendor to capture significant follow-on business. Finally, some schools may be able to negotiate tax-favored contributions.

CONCLUSION

In sum, if the copies made have the effect of increasing the number of simultaneous users of the purchased copy of a program, the fair use section and the computer programs section of the Copyright Act are not satisfactory defenses to charges of infringement. It is outside any concept of fair use to make copies of entire works. Use of such copies by persons other than the owners of purchased copies is outside the scope of Section 117.

However, serial use of the same *owned* copy by more than one teacher or student is permissible. But be careful. Not all program disks are owned copies. Some are leased. Some are loaned. Some are licensed as trade secrets under agreements that restrict use and disclosure in ways probably not possible under copyright licenses as discussed above. Generally, the terms of the lease, loan agreement, or trade secret license, control what the school or teacher may do with the copies.

---

[74] Larson, *Stiffened Software Copyright Protection By Court Isn't Expected to Thwart Pirates,* The Wall Street Jour., Sep. 6, 1983, at 2, col. 3.

[75] Morin, *British Computer Company Takes A Risky Step Into the U.S. Market,* The Wall Street Jour., Sep. 7, 1983, at 33, col. 4.

Insofar as the questions are copyright questions, serial use of non-owned copies is also troublesome. First, Section 117 is not applicable to non-owned copies. Second, while Section 107 is available, the use in question may not be within the Act's conception of "fair use." The argument is that, if the lease or loan agreement is silent, back-up and archival copies are probably "fair use" of the original so long as they are not employed to increase the number of simultaneous users. But that is by no means a clear winner.

To the contrary, back-up and archival copies involve 100% copying, normally outside any conception of "fair use." Indeed, if the making of back-up and archival copies was already within the concept of "fair use," there was really no need expressly to provide for them only as to owned copies in Section 117. Moreover, the relevant portions of Section 117 were drafted when the Section applied to all "lawfully possessed" copies, not just owned copies. Courts may therefore find that back-up and archival copying is not "fair use" based on an interpretation of the Act notwithstanding the overwhelming need to be permitted to do so.

The ultimate practical advice is, of course, the "Golden Rule of Copyright Law" stated at the outset.

September 14, 1983

APPENDIX B
ICCE POLICY STATEMENT ON NETWORK AND MULTIPLE MACHINE SOFTWARE

Just as there has been shared responsibility in the development of this policy, so should there be shared responsibility for resolution of the problems inherent in providing and securing good educational software. Educators have a valid need for quality software and reasonable prices. Hardware developers and/or vendors also must share in the effort to enable educators to make maximum cost-effective use of that equipment. Software authors, developers and vendors are entitled to a fair return on their investment.

Educators' Responsibilities

Educators need to face the legal and ethical issues involved in copyright laws and publisher license agreements and must accept the responsibility for enforcing adherence to these laws and agreements. Budget constraints do not excuse illegal use of software.

Educators should be prepared to provide software developers or their agents with a district-level approved written policy statement including as a minimum:

1. A clear requirement that copyright laws and publisher license agreements be observed;

2. A statement making teachers who use school equipment responsible for taking all reasonable precautions to prevent copying or the use of unauthorized copies on school equipment;
3. An explanation of the steps taken to prevent unauthorized copying or the use of unauthorized copies on school equipment;
4. A designation of who is authorized to sign software license agreements for the school (or district);
5. A designation at the school site level of who is responsible for enforcing the terms of the district policy and terms of licensing agreements;
6. A statement indicating teacher responsibility for educating students about legal, ethical and practical problems caused by illegal use of software.

Hardware Vendors' Responsibilities

Hardware vendors should assist educators in making maximum cost effective use of the hardware and help in enforcing software copyright laws and license agreements. They should as a minimum:

1. Make efforts to see that illegal copies of programs are not being distributed by their employees and agents;
2. Work cooperatively with interested software developers to provide an encryption process which avoids inflexibility but discourages theft.

Software Developers'/Vendors' Responsibilities

Software developers and their agents can share responsibility for helping educators observe copyright laws and publishers' license agreements by developing sales and pricing policies. Software developers and vendors should as a minimum:

1. Provide for all software a back-up copy to be used for archival purposes, to be included with every purchase;
2. Provide for on-approval purchases to allow schools to preview the software to ensure that it meets the needs and expectations of the educational institution. Additionally, software developers are encouraged to provide regional or area centers with software for demonstration purposes. The ICCE encourages educators to develop regional centers for this purpose;

3. Work in cooperation with hardware vendors to provide an encryption process which avoids inflexibility but discourages theft;
4. Provide for, and note in advertisements, multiple-copy pricing for school sites with several machines and recognize that multiple copies do not necessarily call for multiple documentation;
5. Provide for, and note in advertisements, network-compatible versions of software with pricing structures that recognize the extra costs of developing to secure compatibility and recognize the buyer's need for only a single copy of the software.

The Board of Directors of The International Council for Computers in Education approved this policy statement, with attachments, June 5, 1983.

The committee that drafted this policy included:

Jenny Better, Director of Curriculum, Cupertino Union Elementary District
LeRoy Finkel, San Mateo County Office of Education
Pennie Gallant, Apple Computer, Inc.
John Hazelwood/Jeffrey Armstrong, Corvus Systems, Inc.
Marion B. Kenworthy, Saratoga High School
Richard R. Monnard, Addison-Wesley Publishing Co.
Henry Vigil/Cliff Godwin, Cybertronics International
William Wagner, Santa Clara County Office of Education

ATTACHMENT 1

Suggested District Policy on Software Copyright

It is the intent of__________________________________ to adhere to the provisions of copyright laws in the area of microcomputer programs. Though there continues to be controversy regarding interpretation of those copyright laws, the following procedures represent a sincere effort to operate legally. We recognize that computer software piracy is a major problem for the industry and that violations of computer copyright laws contribute to higher costs and greater efforts to prevent copies and/or lessen incentives for the development of good educational software. All of these results are detrimental to the development of effective educational uses of microcomputers. Therefore, in an effort to discourage violation of copyright laws and to prevent such illegal activities:

1. The ethical and practical problems caused by software piracy will be taught in all schools in the District.
2. District employees will be expected to adhere to the provisions of Public Law 96-517, Section 7(b) which amends Section 117 of Title 17 of the United States Code to allow for the making of a back-up copy of computer programs. This states that " . . . it is not an infringement for the owner of a copy of a computer program to make or authorize the making of another copy or adaptation of that computer program provided:
   a. that such a new copy or adaptation is created as an essential step in the utilization of the computer program in conjunction with a machine and that it is used in no other manner, or
   b. that such a new copy and adaptation is for archival purposes only and that all archival copies are destroyed in the event that continued possession of the computer program should cease to be rightful."
3. When software is to be used on a disk sharing system, efforts will be made to secure this software from copying.
4. Illegal copies of copyrighted programs may not be made or used on school equipment.
5. The legal or insurance protection of the District will not be extended to employees who violate copyright laws.
6. ________________________________ of this school district is designated as the only individual who may sign license agreements for software for schools in the district. (Each school using the software also should have a signature on a copy of the software agreement for local control.)
7. The principal of each school site is responsible for establishing practices which will enforce this policy at the school level.

ATTACHMENT 2

Sample Software Policy of a Community College with a Large Microcomputer Lab

It is the policy of this college that no person shall use or cause to be used in the college's microcomputer laboratories any software which does not fall into one of the following categories:

1. It is in the public domain.
2. It is covered by a licensing agreement with the software author, authors, vendor or developer, whichever is applicable.
3. It has been donated to the college and a written record of a bona fide contribution exists.
4. It has been purchased by the college and a record of a bona fide purchase exists.
5. It has been purchased by the user and a record of a bona fide purchase exists and can be produced by the user upon demand.
6. It is being reviewed or demonstrated by the users in order to reach a decision about possible future purchase or request for contribution or licensing.
7. It has been written or developed by ____________________ (college employee) for the specific purpose of being used in the ____________________(college) microcomputer laboratory.

It is also the policy of the college that there be no copying of copyrighted or proprietary programs on computers belonging to the college.

Source: De Anza College, Cupertino, California.

ATTACHMENT 3
Suggested Format of Software Licenses

1. Designated on a per site, district-wide or other geographic basis.
2. Requires the signature of a responsible school employee.
3. Includes provisions for a single copy purchase (with archival back-up copy) at full price.
4. Multiple-machine pricing:
   Includes provisions for a quantity discount for subsequent purchases of the same software provided:
   a. the purchase discount applies to a single purchase order.
   b. the purchase discount is noncumulative.
   c. the software is for the same computer type.

   i.e.: Radio Shack presently offers a 50% discount for purchases of 10 or more sets of the same software; Gregg/McGraw-Hill offers a discount schedule with incremental increases—buy 2, pay 10% or less; 3—20% less; 4—30% less; 5 or more, 40% less.

5. Network Pricing:
   May be offered as per school site or with quantity discount for school districts with multiple sites. Provide for a flat license fee for network-compatible versions of the software.
   - flat fee provision is preferred over any variable rate based on number of computers or number of student users.
   - network-compatibility, not just an unlocked version of the software, is required to eliminate the need for local re-programming of copyrighted and licensed software.

   Include provision for purchase of multiple copies of documentation and accompanying materials. i.e.: A flat fee of two times the single copy retail price is offered to network users of Random House software.

ATTACHMENT 4
Some Technical Notes on Software Encryption for Software/Hardware Vendors

1. Single Machine Encryption

Explanation:

The purchased disk is not copiable by ordinary means. The software cannot be transferred to network system or used on several computers at once. This scheme is the most common, especially for inexpensive software.

Technical Notes:

The protected disk is usually formatted in a non-standard way which will defeat standard disk copy programs such as COPY A on the Apple or TRSDOS BACKUP on the TRS-80. Alternatively, the publisher may write special information on the disk in places which the standard disk copy programs do not check. The copy program proceeds to completion, but the special information is not transferred to the duplicate disk. When the duplicate is used, the software checks for the special information, fails to find it, and stops.

Implications:
Schools will need to purchase many copies of the same program and should expect significant volume discounts. The customer is entitled to an archival backup and should expect the publisher to include a backup disk with every purchase.
Manufacturers of network systems should recognize that single machine encryption (which is incompatible with their products) will remain the software industry standard unless they actively support software protection on their systems.

2. Single Site Encryption

Explanation:
A single product can serve all the machines at a site. This scheme applies to VisiCalc™ and Logo.

Technical Notes:
Software which loads initially into memory and subsequently interacts only with data disks is de facto "single site encrypted," even though the program disk may be uncopiable. A single program disk can be used to initialize all the computers in a room, after which each user operates with his or her own data disks. VisiCalc™ and Logo operate in this way.
A functionally equivalent alternative is referred to as "master and slave" or "lock and key" encryption. This scheme is common where a program is too large to fit in memory all at once. Frequent disk access is needed as different parts of the software are brought into play.
In the "lock and key" scheme, the program modules which are routinely needed can be freely copied. A "slave" disk containing these modules is duplicated for each computer (or even for each student). The slave will not operate, however, unless the computer has been cold started with the (uncopiable) master disk.

Implications:
Since the "master" disk is uncopiable, the publisher still bears the burden of providing an archival backup. The protection on the "master" disk normally makes the software incompatible with network systems, so the above comments again apply.

Single site encryption reduces the dependence on volume discounts to facilitate multiple machine use. However, volume discounts should still be made available at the district level to encourage district level adoption of software.

3. **Hard Disk/Network Compatible Versions of Software**

Explanation:

Floppy disks containing network compatible software must be copiable since the software is copied as it is transferred onto the network. The problem of protecting network compatible software is how to allow this legitimate copying while preventing illegal copying.

One solution is to abandon software protection altogether and to rely on license agreements to prevent illegal use of the program(s). The problem with this solution is that freely copiable software may be freely copied.

Other solutions rely on publishing special versions of the software for the various network systems available. These versions do not run on stand-alone computers.

A publisher can also take steps to discourage people from installing the network software at sites other than the intended site.

Technical Notes:

A publisher can prevent network software from running on a stand-alone computer by using a device check. The software senses whether it is running on a network system and stops if it is not. The device check is specific to the network system involved. Software with a device check could be installed at many network sites, not just the one for which it was licensed.

To discourage use at non-license sites, the publisher can embed the name of the license in the software. This requires that the publisher customize each network-compatible version sold. Although such customization discourages porting the software to another network site, it does not physically prevent it.

To prevent porting of the software to another network, the publisher might implement what is essentially single machine encryption on the network level. This protection scheme would work by checking the serial number or other unique indentifier in the network hardware. If the software encountered a change in identifier, it would fail to operate. This has the disadvantages that a licensee would have to be a single network installation and that normal activities such as replacing or upgrading one's network system would disable the software.

Implications:

Use of a device check requires a publisher to maintain a separate inventory item for each device to be supported. The time required for a publisher to embed the customer's name in each product sold for use on networks can become prohibitive.

These protection schemes may prove economically unfeasible for inexpensive software.

These protection schemes require close working relationships and sharing of information between publishers and network system manufacturers.

APPENDIX C

AGREEMENT ON GUIDELINES FOR CLASSROOM COPYING IN NOT-FOR-PROFIT EDUCATIONAL INSTITUTIONS

WITH RESPECT TO BOOKS AND PERIODICALS

The purpose of the following guidelines is to state the minimum standards of educational fair use under Section 107 of H.R. 2223. The parties agree that the conditions determining the extent of permissible copying for educational purposes may change in the future; that certain types of copying permitted under these guidelines may not be permissible in the future; and conversely that in the future other types of copying not permitted under these guidelines may be permissible under revised guidelines.

Moreover, the following statement of guidelines is not intended to limit the types of copying permitted under the standards of fair use under judicial decision and which are stated in Section 107 of the Copyright Revision Bill. There may be instances in which copying which does not fall within the guidelines stated below may nonetheless be permitted under the criteria of fair use.

GUIDELINES

I. Single Copying for Teachers.

A single copy may be made of any of the following by or for a teacher at his or her individual request for his or her scholarly research or use in teaching or preparation to teach a class:

A. A chapter from a book;

B. An article from a periodical or newspaper;

C. A short story, short essay or short poem, whether or not from a collective work;

D. A chart, graph, diagram, drawing, cartoon or picture from a book, periodical, or newspaper;

II. Multiple Copies for Classroom Use

Multiple copies (not to exceed in any event more than one copy per pupil in a course) may be made by or for the teacher giving the course for classroom use or discussion; *provided that:*

A. The copying meets the tests of brevity and spontaneity as defined below; *and,*

B. Meets the cumulative effect test as defined below; *and,*

C. Each copy includes a notice of copyright.

Definitions

Brevity

(*i*) Poetry: (a) A complete poem if less than 250 words and if printed on not more than two pages or, (b) from a longer poem, an excerpt of not more than 250 words.

(*ii*) Prose: (a) Either a complete article, story or essay of less than 2,500 words, or (b) an excerpt from any prose work of not more than 1,000 words or 10% of the work, whichever is less, but in any event a minimum of 500 words.

[Each of the numerical limits stated in "i" and "ii" above may be expanded to permit the completion of an unfinished line of a poem or of an unfinished prose paragraph.]

(*iii*) Illustration: One chart, graph, diagram, drawing, cartoon or picture per book or per periodical issue.

(*iv*) "Special" works: Certain works in poetry, prose or in "poetic prose" which often combine language with illustrations and which are intended sometimes for children and at other times for a more general audience fall short of 2,500 words in their entirety. Paragraph "ii" above notwithstanding such "special works" may not be reproduced in their entirety; however, an excerpt comprising not more than two of the published pages of such special work and containing not more than 10% of the words found in the text thereof, may be reproduced.

Spontaneity

(*i*) The copying is at the instance and inspiration of the individual teacher, and

(*ii*) The inspiration and decision to use the work and the moment of its use for maximum teaching effectiveness are so close in time that it would be unreasonable to expect a timely reply to a request for permission.

Cumulative Effect

(*i*) The copying of the material is for only one course in the school in which the copies are made.

(*ii*) Not more than one short poem, article, story, essay or two excerpts may be copied from the same author, nor more than three from the same collective work or periodical volume during one class term.

(*iii*) There shall not be more than nine instances of such multiple copying for one course during one class term.

[The limitations stated in "ii" and "iii" above shall not apply to current news periodicals and newspapers and current news sections of other periodicals.]

III. Prohibitions as to I and II Above

Notwithstanding any of the above, the following shall be prohibited:

(A) Copying shall not be used to create or to replace or substitute for anthologies, compilations or collective works. Such replacement or substitution may occur whether copies of various works or excerpts therefrom are accumulated or reproduced and used separately.

(B) There shall be no copying of or from works intended to be "consumable" in the course of study or of teaching. These include workbooks, exercises, standardized tests and test booklets and answer sheets and like consumable material.

(C) Copying shall not:

(a) substitute for the purchase of books, publishers' reprints or periodicals;

(b) be directed by higher authority;

(c) be repeated with respect to the same item by the same teacher from term to term.

(D) No charge shall be made to the student beyond the actual cost of the photocopying.

Agreed MARCH 19, 1976.

Ad Hoc Committee on Copyright Law Revision:

By SHELDON ELLIOTT STEINBACH.

Author-Publisher Group:

Authors League of America:

By IRWIN KARP, *Counsel.*

Association of American Publishers, Inc.:

By ALEXANDER C. HOFFMAN,
Chairman, Copyright Committee.

APPENDIX D

GUIDELINES FOR OFF-AIR RECORDING OF BROADCAST PROGRAMMING FOR EDUCATIONAL PURPOSES

1. The guidelines were developed to apply only to off-air recording by nonprofit educational institutions.
2. A broadcast program may be recorded off-air simultaneously with broadcast transmission (including simultaneous cable retransmission) and retained by a nonprofit educational institution for a period not to exceed the first forty-five (45) consecutive calendar days after date of recording. Upon conclusion of such retention period, all off-air recordings must be erased or destroyed immediately. "Broadcast programs" are television programs transmitted by television stations for reception by the general public without charge.
3. Off-air recordings may be used once by individual teachers in the course of relevant teaching activities, and repeated once only when instructional reinforcement is necessary, in classrooms and similar places devoted to instruction within a single building, cluster, or campus, as well as in the homes of students receiving formalized home instruction, during the first ten (10) consecutive school days in the forty-five (45) day calendar day retention period. "School days" are school session days—not counting weekends, holidays, vacations, examination periods, or other

scheduled interruptions—within the forty-five (45) calendar day retention period.

4. Off-air recordings may be made only at the request of and used by individual teachers, and may not be regularly recorded in anticipation of requests. No broadcast program may be recorded off-air more than once at the request of the same teacher, regardless of the number of times the program may be broadcast.
5. A limited number of copies may be reproduced from each off-air recording to meet the legitimate needs of teachers under these guidelines. Each such additional copy shall be subject to all provisions governing the original recording.
6. After the first ten (10) consecutive school days, off-air recordings may be used up to the end of the forty-five (45) calendar days retention period only for teacher evaluation purposes, i.e., to determine whether or not to include the broadcast program in the teaching curriculum, and may not be used in the recording institution for student exhibition or any other nonevaluation purpose without authorization.
7. Off-air recordings need not be used in their entirety, but the recorded programs may not be altered from their original content. Off-air recordings may not be physically or electronically combined or merged to constitute teaching anthologies or compilations.
8. All copies of off-air recordings must include the copyright notice on the broadcast program as recorded.
9. Educational institutions are expected to establish appropriate control procedures to maintain the integrity of these guidelines.

APPENDIX E

THE SCHOOL BOARD OF SARASOTA COUNTY

MEMORANDUM

TO:	Members of the School Board Dr. James H. Fox, Jr., Superintendent
FROM:	Warren L. Spurlin, Deputy Superintendent
DATE:	October 24, 1983
RE:	Request for Approval of Policy/Regulation 3223.1 and Policy/Regulation 3223.2

As per School Board direction, Policy/Regulation 3223.1 regarding Computer Software Copyright Negotiation and Policy-Regulation 3223.2 regarding Computer Software Copyright have been advertised.

The administration is now requesting approval of these Policies/ Regulations. We have had no negative comments as of this date.

If you have any questions please give me a call.

WLS:b
attachments

Suggestion Motion: I move approval of Policy/Regulation 3223.1 and Policy/Regulation 3223.2 as presented.

PURCHASING SERVICES—BIDS AND QUOTATIONS

Computer Software Copyright Negotiations—3223.1

All Sarasota County School District personnel involved in the selection and purchase of Computer Software and ancillary consumable materials must negotiate with prospective vendors or suppliers to gain a release, or favorable reduction, in copyright limitations before any recommendation to purchase is made. This negotiation must be documented and presented to their immediate administrative supervisor for concurrence before the purchase order is prepared.

Documentation should include responses from a vendors management level representative and should have commitments to release stated in writing.

Software purchase recommendations for curriculum and instruction use must have the prior approval of the Associate Superintendent for Instructional Services or his designee(s).

Software purchase recommendations for other areas must have the prior approval of the Deputy Superintendent or his designee(s).

Specific documentation of negotiation results will be presented to the Director of Purchasing in the prescribed format. Variations and deviations will be reviewed by the Deputy Superintendent.

Computer Software Copyright—3223.2

The Instructional Division will develop an instructional process to assist in teaching ethical and practical issues related to computer software development and use.

District employees are to become familiar with and adhere to statutes relative to computer program and software copyrights. Specifically, the provision of P.L. 96-517, Section 7(b) which amends Section 117 of Title 7 of the United States Code to allow for making backup copies of computer programs will be printed and given to each district employee associated with computer and computer program activity. Authorization component:

a. that such a new copy or adaptation is created as an essential step in the utilization of the computer program in conjunction with a machine and that it is used in no other manner, or
b. that such a new copy and adaptation is for archival purposes only and that all archival copies are destroyed in the event that continued possession of the computer program should cease to be rightful.

Employees are advised of the following guidelines and are accountable for awareness and compliance.

a. When software is to be used on a disk sharing system, efforts will be made to secure this software from copying.
b. Illegal copies of copyrighted programs may not be made or used on school equipment.
c. The legal or insurance protection of the District will not be extended to employees who violate copyright laws.
d. The Director of Purchasing after authorization from the Associate Superintendent for Instructional Services or the Deputy Superintendent is designated as the only individual who may sign license agreements for software for schools in the district. (Each school using the software also will have a signature on a copy of the software agreement for local control.)
e. The principal of each school site is responsible for establishing practices which will enforce this policy at the school level. Similar rules will be established for central administrative cost centers.

PURCHASING—Soliciting Prices

Computer Software Copyright Negotiation—3223.1

It shall be the policy of the Sarasota County School District to negotiate for specific copyright release with vendors or suppliers of all computer software and consumable support materials. Written evidence of this negotiation shall be presented to the Director of Purchasing prior to the purchase. Where releases are not obtained alternative products will be considered before purchasing from a non-cooperating vendor.

Computer Software Copyright—3223.2

It is the intent of The School Board of Sarasota County to adhere to the provisions of copyright laws in all areas including micro-computer programs and computer software. Computer software piracy is a major problem for the industry. Violations of computer copyright laws contribute to higher costs. Therefore, in an effort to encourage compliance with copyright laws specific regulations will define appropriate procedures to follow.

APPENDIX F

SAMPLE LICENSING AGREEMENTS

Program Copyright © 1982 by John Conrad.
Documentation Copyright © 1982 by Edu-Ware Services, Inc.
All Rights Reserved. Any reproduction of the program diskette, or this printed documentation is strictly forbidden, without the expressed written consent of Edu-Ware Services, Inc.

WARNING: Subject to the provisions of the copyright act of 1980, as specified in Public Law 94-553, dated 12 December, 1980 (94 STAT. 3028-29) and amended as Public Law 96-517, the duplication of computer programs without prior consent of the publisher, for the purpose of barter, trade, sale or exchange is a criminal offense, for which the offender may be subject to fine, imprisonment, and/or civil suit. Under the provisions of Section 117 of Public Law 96-517 it is not an infringement for the owner of a computer program to make or authorize the making of another copy or adaptation of that computer program provided that such new copy or adaptation is created for archival purposes only and that all archival copies are destroyed in the event that continued possession of the computer program should cease to be rightful.

Spelling Bee Games was developed exclusively by John Conrad in cooperation with Edu-Ware Services, Inc., a California software development company dedicated to the production of instructionally valid Computer Assisted Instruction and intellectually challenging games.

EDU-WARE has elected to use the pronoun HE when addressing a mixed audience. We have considered the alternatives and we have chosen traditional usage for clarity and readability.

Copyright 1982, Software Productions, Inc.
P.O. Box 21341, Columbus, Ohio 43221.

This software product and all documentation and enclosures are copyrighted and all rights are reserved by Software Productions, Inc. This product may not, in whole or in part, be copied, photocopied, reproduced, translated or reduced to any electronic medium, or machine readable form without prior consent, in writing from Software Productions, Inc.

Your "Micro Mother Goose" disk is not copy-protected.

We know from experience that any software frequently used by children has a good chance of coming down with a fatal case of fingerprints or the "peanut butter and jellies." So we feel that parents and teachers should be able to make a "just in case" back-up copy of "Micro Mother Goose."

We suggest that you immediately make a copy of your "Micro Mother Goose" disk with the RUN COPYA program on your System Master disk (explained on page 38 of "The DOS Manual"). Use the copied disk as your "working" disk. Store your original "Micro Mother Goose" disk in a safe place so if an accident occurs, you can use it to make another copy.

We think the ability to easily replace disks damaged by normal family or classroom wear and tear is a real benefit. Now you won't have to fuss with the inconvenience of complicated disk replacement procedures. You won't have to buy another "Micro Mother Goose" package. And you won't have to spend frustrating hours trying to "break" a complicated copy protection scheme just to get a back-up copy.

This is NOT a license to steal, otherwise known as "software piracy." The copying of "Micro Mother Goose" for purposes other than for a personal back-up copy is just plain stealing which is illegal. Adults should think twice before they steal "Micro Mother Goose." Parents and teachers who engage in this kind of unethical behavior are setting a very poor example for their children.

By the way, we've included an extra disk label in this package which you can use on your "working" copy of "Micro Mother Goose."

Our goal is to provide the best in "Classic Family Software" for you. Feel free to write us with your comments and suggestions. Many Thanks!

"Micro Mother Goose" is fully guaranteed. If it ever fails to boot, for any reason whatever, return the disk to Software Productions for a free replacement. If the disk has been physically damaged, please include five dollars for a replacement disk.

The graphics in "Micro Mother Goose" were created with The Graphics Magician. The Graphics Magician was written by Mark Pelczarski, David Lubar and Chris Jochumson and is published by Penquin Software.

---

1 Mill Street
Burlington, Vermont 05401
(802) 862-7355

In Search of The Most Amazing Thing™
was created by **Tom Snyder Productions, Inc.**
Cambridge, Massachusetts